Recipes from a Provençal Kitchen

Michel Biehn

Recipes from a Provençal Kitchen

Photographs
by Bernard Touillon

~

Translated by
Antony & Christine Grant

Mitchell Beazley

For Paul and Jeanne

First published in Great Britain in 1995
by Mitchell Beazley
an imprint of Reed Consumer Books Limited
Michelin House, 81 Fulham Road
London SW3 6RB
and Auckland, Melbourne, Singapore and Toronto
English translation copyright © Reed Consumer Books
Translated by Antony & Christine Grant
Originally published in 1994 by Flammarion
as *Le Cahier de Recettes Provençales*

Copyright © Flammarion 1994

A CIP catalogue record for this book
is available from the British Library.

ISBN 1 85732 610 5
Printed and bound in Germany

Editorial director Ghislaine Bavoillot
Art director Marc Walter

contents

— 7 —
THE SIMPLICITY OF
MY GRANDMOTHER'S COOKING

— 17 —
AUTUMN SQUASH

— 35 —
CABBAGE AND ROMANCE

— 45 —
TEATIME IN THE KITCHEN

— 59 —
A CHRISTMAS SUPPER IN PROVENCE

— 71 —
FROM CHRISTMAS TO THE NEW YEAR

— 77 —
UNDER A WINTER'S SUN

— 93 —
A SPRING LUNCH

— 111 —
BREAKFAST WITH THE HORSEMEN

— 123 —
BOUILLABAISSE IN
AN ARTIST'S STUDIO

— 139 —
A PICNIC ON THE BANKS OF THE
RIVER SORGUE

— 151 —
A DAY AT THE 'CABANON'

— 167 —
LUNCH ON THE TERRACE

— 183 —
A GARDEN FEAST

The Simplicity of My Grandmother's Cooking

Like my father I have always loved food. When my parents were married in 1947 in Arles, my grandmother, Athalie Pascal, armed with ink and pen, copied into a school notebook the recipes she had learnt from her mother. In another book were inscribed her pastry and dessert recipes. She gave these recipes to her daughter on her wedding day, as she had done for my Uncle Victor and my Aunt Elisabeth a few years earlier. I have those notebooks with me now and many of the recipes in this book, the added touches, a 'small carrot' here, a 'sprig of thyme' there, come from the subtle *savoir-faire* of that beautiful and generous woman, brought up in Sault, who was my grandmother.

My mother very quickly added her own personal touches to the notebook recipes. This delighted her husband, her son and her friends, for she developed a style of cooking that was both simple and refined, in the Provençal tradition, but also quite often enriched with butter and cream, which my father adored, for he was from Alsace. I was often in the kitchen with my mother. I adored watching her work and from time to time, she even let me help.

As a child, one of my great joys on Christmas Eve was to prepare the almonds for the Yule log. It was a task I undertook almost religiously. First, I had to break the shells, then blanch the nuts in a pan of boiling water. Then I skinned the nuts and dried them in a cloth. I spread them in a small metal dish which had two brass handles. The dish went into a slow oven where the almonds were roasted until golden, but not burnt. Then, while they were still hot, I would place them between two sheets of thick paper and with all my might I would crush them into a powder with a rolling pin. There is nothing I remember with greater pleasure than the aroma rising from the nuts at that moment.

Athalie Pascal's recipe notebook

Now I, too, have filled a notebook with recipes, a large white book covered in cloth embroidered with blue and yellow silks, bought at the flea market. In it, over the years, I have recorded the exotic culinary discoveries of my friends, and the wonderful memories of all the meals shared with the people dear to me. They have shaped my love of good food, and considerably added to my own knowledge of cooking.

In Arles, in the old days, when a woman was in her everyday clothes, she was said to be in a dress of 'simplicity' as compared with the more elaborate one worn on Sundays. In the same way, one can think of Provençal cooking as *une cuisine de simplicité*. If in Provence we cook elaborate dishes prepared with puff pastry, sauces and mousses, we are not being true to the Provençal tradition. This is *la cuisine bourgeoise*, 'as found in Paris'. Provençal cooking derives its original flavours from the marvellous products either grown, raised or found in Provence or near its coasts: anchovies, *tellines* (our own brand of cockles), cardoons, purple artichokes, garlic, olives, almonds and truffles. Cooking techniques are mainly simple: grilling, baking and boiling are the methods used, with a few simmered dishes such as *la daube* and *la barigoule*. The only sauces used are *le coulis de*

tomates, *la rouille* and *l'aïoli*, and more often than not, just a dash of olive oil. For dessert, some fresh *brousse* cheese with jam, or simply fruit, since we believe that Provence grows the most beautiful fruit on earth. Provençal cooking is also seasonal cooking, using fresh ingredients bought from the market when they are in their prime. Courgettes are best in the summer and asparagus at Easter. No cans, except for tomatoes, because when you have to make a tomato *coulis* in December, canned tomatoes are preferable to those tasteless greenhouse tomatoes for which you pay a fortune.

What makes this cuisine unique and subtle is the refined, artistic, almost scientific way the people of Provence have of enhancing flavours with vegetables, herbs and spices, and of blending them together. For example the leek, when it is not used as a main vegetable in a dish, is often added for flavour in small quantities to fish recipes, especially salt cod. This is equally true of carrots and olives in recipes for meat stews. Anchovies also play an important role in many dishes and they enhance beautifully the flavour of our Easter leg of kid, as well as that of a Christmas cardoon gratin.

Above all, it is my mission to refute the heresy that *herbes de Provence* are the

Flowering thyme

basic flavours of Provence. Cooking *à la Provençale* does not mean dipping into a big bag of mixed herbs and throwing them on grilled meats and roasts, or into sauces or stews. That is an old wives' tale. But a sprig of thyme, a bay leaf or a piece of orange rind, sometimes together, sometimes separate, will definitely flavour *une daube* or *un coulis* in the Provençal way.

There is one more ingredient that deserves a special mention and that is grated cheese. In Provence, we just call it *le râpé*. We serve it with all the soups and it covers most gratins, with or without breadcrumbs. In the past, Dutch cheese was used, which we used to call *le rouge* (it was Edam with annatto colouring) – then Gruyère arrived and completely replaced *le rouge*. I personally think that it's a pity and that we should go back to the old ways and use *le rouge* on *soupe au pistou*, for instance.

As we have talked about cheese, I would like to say a few words about bread. Everywhere in Provence, the bread is excellent and our bakers are real artists. They have the know-how to create a great variety of shapes and textures, and they have given them lovely names like *l'épi* and *le fendu*, *la couronne* and *la fougasse*, *le pain d'Aix* and *le petit Beaucaire*.

Of course, I must also mention the delicious wines of Provence – the *rosés* of Palette and Bandol, of Ventoux and the Luberon – that one drinks chilled in the summer. We also have superb reds from Gigondas and Aix-en-Provence and whites from Cassis and Châteauneuf-du-Pape, not to mention the muscat from Beaumes-de-Venise. Every time it seemed appropriate, I have suggested one of these wines to accompany the recipes in this book.

As you will have guessed by now, I love this part of the world, its food and its customs, and I hope you will want to share that passion. But as I have already told you, my father was from Alsace, and a lover of good food, and I must admit that his influence has slightly perverted an otherwise fairly strict family tradition when it comes to cooking. So do not be surprised if my dessert and pastry recipes seem a little richer than Provençal simplicity would usually allow. Apart from these few exceptions, and some exotic inclusions suggested by friends, I do try to be a faithful follower of that beautiful Provençal tradition. Nevertheless, this book doesn't pretend to be an exhaustive, historical or ethnological study of the culinary habits and customs of Provençal cooks, nor is it an instruction manual, so that although you will find all the details

'Le

Pages 1
Athalie Pa
recipe note

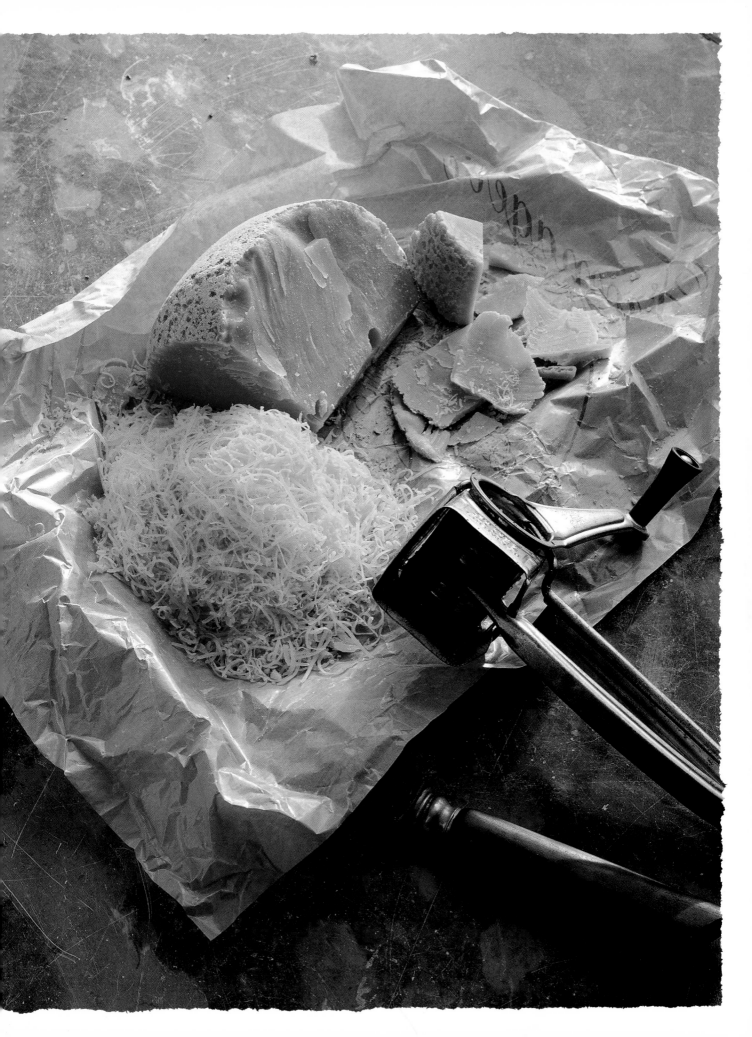

necessary to prepare the recipes, I have not included a list of ingredients, nor have I organized the recipes by type.

$\qquad$ This book is first and foremost a gathering of friends. I wanted to take you on a gourmet tour of a house, a dream house which would have a terrace overlooking the sea, as well as a garden along the Sorgue, a big yellow living-room and a small red drawing-room, a spiral staircase going up to the attic, a stately kitchen and a vegetable garden, a window opening on to the Camargue and another on to Mount Ventoux.

In welcoming me into their homes, my friends have allowed me to make this dream house come true. So, we will go to the Château de l'Ange in Lumières, the house of Michel and Edith Mézard, for a candlelit dinner for two and a garden feast. The afternoon tea will be served in the superb kitchen of the Château d'Ansouis, the home of Géraud and Stéphanette de Sabran-Pontèves. We will celebrate Christmas at Vinsobres, at Jean and Hélène Feraud's house. Lillian Williams will let us lunch with the Chinese mandarins in the main living room of her magnificent *bastide* near Aix-en-Provence. Jack Grange will welcome us in his exotic garden overlooking the Alpilles. Then we'll share lunch with *les gardians* (horsemen) in the heart of the Camargue at Henri, Annie and Patrick Laurent's *mas des Marquises*. We'll spend a day in a creek, at Denis Savon's *cabanon* (cabin). Finally, we'll dine happily under Bruno Carles' veranda at Lunel, and Gérard Drouillet will prepare a *bouillabaisse* in his studio in Eygalières. For each of these magical places, I have chosen a special time of year and I have organized the recipes in Athalie's notebook according to the passing of the seasons.

This book is a very personal vision of the simple and beautiful way the people of Provence enjoy each other's company. It makes each moment of life happy, and in perfect harmony with the climate, the countryside and the light of Provence.

'Le rouge'

*Breads f
Provence:
and le fendu
fougasse, le p
d'Aix and le p
Beauc*

AUTUMN SQUASH

It's autumn in Provence. The tourists, a little sad, are going home and our village squares have stopped being ugly parking lots and returned to their usual peace and quiet. Summer lingers on, the air is exquisitely mild, and the light, oblique and clear, is more beautiful than ever. Still, the leaves are falling from the trees and the days are shorter. The garden is turning yellow with the lime trees and red with the ripening persimmons. In the morning, after the mist has lifted, one can pick the last tomatoes, the ones that will never ripen, with which to make jam. In the pine trees the *cigales* (cicadas) have stopped singing until next summer, while on the kitchen walls their well-behaved ceramic cousins seem to enjoy the aromas coming from a pumpkin transformed into a lovely soup tureen and filled with a delicious thick bread soup, or those from the large green cabbage which has been stuffed and re-formed into its beautiful rounded shape. In the oven, the pieces of rabbit in mustard sauce are roasting nicely. The crusts are forming on the gratins, and the potatoes are swelling and turning golden. On a baking sheet, the candied orange and lemon rinds are drying along with the large sheets of quince paste. Meanwhile, soft chocolate fudge is hardening on a marble slab before being wrapped in silver paper. It is autumn in our kitchen at l'Isle-sur-la-Sorgue. Welcome.

umpkin
nd Bread
oup

Pages 18–19:
The kitchen
with cicadas

Pumpkin and
Bread Soup

~

The pumpkin we grow around here is called 'nutmeg' pumpkin. Its rind is a milky caramel colour – less red than that of some pumpkins – its flesh bright orange, sweet and full of flavour. In the pumpkin family it is rather small, much smaller than the celebrated pumpkin which, on fairytale nights, is transformed into Cinderella's carriage. We harvest pumpkins in the autumn and, as with apples, as long as they are unblemished they keep all winter.

Here is a beautiful soup, one in which the pumpkin will play all the parts: the soup tureen and the soup, the dish and the meal, the decanter and the wine. Don't laugh, wait until you've tried it!

IN THE KITCHEN : Choose a nice unblemished pumpkin, weighing 3 to 4 kg (6 to 8 lb). Cut out a lid in the top – a large hole – through which a ladle can pass easily. With a spoon, remove and discard all the seeds and the fibres surrounding them. Fill the inside of the pumpkin with small cubes of dry bread and grated cheese, and 1–2 garlic cloves, finely chopped. Season with sea salt and freshly ground pepper. Then pour in fairly liquid fresh double cream, enough to cover the bread – to about 2.5 cm (1 inch) from the top. Put the lid back on the pumpkin, wrap it in aluminium foil and bake for 2 hours in a fairly hot oven.

Taking the pumpkin out of the oven can be tricky because the skin will have softened during cooking. Be careful not to let it collapse. Remove the aluminium foil and let the pumpkin drain for a while. Then put it in a deep dish and remove the lid. With a wooden spoon, carefully scrape away the cooked flesh, not too close to the skin, and mix it with the cream and bread. For a smooth soup, the mixture will need to be puréed. Ladle this thick and delicious soup into warmed bowls.

Stuffed Pumpkin

~

For this recipe you will need a small pumpkin about 20 cm (8 inches) in diameter. Cut out a lid in the top and remove the seeds and the fibres surrounding them. Using a spoon, scoop out the flesh. You will need only about half of it – the remainder can go into a good vegetable soup. Chop up the flesh with 2 garlic cloves and a generous bunch of parsley, and then fry in olive oil until well cooked; season with salt, pepper and a pinch of sugar. Chop up 500 g (1 lb) of leftover cooked meat (beef, pork or lamb will do nicely) with a little bread that has been soaked in milk and then drained. Mix together the meat and pumpkin, and bind the mixture with 2 beaten eggs, a large tablespoon of fresh single cream, and 125 g (4 oz) of grated cheese. Stuff the pumpkin shell with this mixture, to not more than 2.5 cm (1 inch) from the top as it swells during cooking. Replace the lid, and wrap the pumpkin in aluminium foil. Cook in a hot oven for about 2 hours.

Do not be surprised if it takes as long to cook this small pumpkin as the large pumpkin used in the previous recipe – this is because the meat stuffing requires a little more time to cook. Once ready, take out of the oven, carefully remove the aluminium foil and allow the pumpkin to drain for a while before serving in a deep dish.

WINE :
Coteaux
de Pierrevert
rouge

Pumpkin and
Spinach Tian

~

A *tian* is a glazed earthenware dish in which we prepare gratins in the oven. I say 'in the oven' now that everyone has one. *Tians* traditionally were cooked at the bakers or, if one lived too far from the village, in the fireplace, covered with a sheet of corrugated iron bearing hot coals. So *tian* is the name of a ceramic dish, but as with *terrine* and *marmite*, it has also become the name of its contents. In more contemporary French, we say gratin.

There are *tians* or gratins of almost everything – from vegetables to fish, fruit and even milk – since this cooking method is so common in a typical Provençal kitchen.

But let us start with a *tian* of pumpkin and spinach. The colour and flavour of these two vegetables complement each other perfectly, and this gratin is a truly exquisite dish.

IN THE KITCHEN : You will need 1 kg (2 lb) of young spinach, thoroughly washed. Discard the stalks and the larger veins, and blanch the leaves in lightly salted boiling water for about 3 minutes. Drain well and use the leaves to line a buttered gratin dish. Cover with 2 table-spoons of fresh double cream and some freshly ground black pepper. Meanwhile, take 1 kg (2 lb) of pumpkin flesh and cut into cubes. Cook the pumpkin in a little olive oil, with salt, pepper and a pinch of sugar, in a covered pan over a low heat until tender, which will take about 30 minutes. Using a fork, mash the pumpkin together with 1 tablespoon of flour and 2 egg yolks. Beat the 2 egg whites until stiff, and carefully fold into the pumpkin. Spoon the pumpkin mixture on to the spinach leaves. Sprinkle with some grated Gruyère cheese and cook in a hot oven for about 15 minutes, or until the cheese has melted and is bubbling. Serve immediately.

Pumpkin and Rice Tian

~

Peel a slice of pumpkin weighing 1.5 kg (3 lb) and cut into cubes. Cook in a covered frying pan over a low heat with 1 tablespoon of olive oil, a drop of water, some sea salt, some freshly ground pepper and a pinch of sugar, until the pumpkin is very tender. Stir with a wooden spoon from time to time. In the meantime, boil 1 cup of Camargue round rice (short-grain rice) in lightly salted water for about 15 minutes. Mix the well-drained rice with the mashed pumpkin, and place in an ovenproof gratin dish.
Sprinkle with some grated Gruyère cheese, breadcrumbs and a few drops of olive oil. Cook in a hot oven for a good 15 minutes, or until the cheese has melted. Allow the *tian* to cool slightly before serving.

Large and Small
Stuffed Cabbages
~

Choose a large round cabbage, firm and tight, weighing at least 1 kg (2 lb). Discard the outer leaves. Separate and wash all of the remaining leaves, keeping aside the small leaves of the cabbage heart, and blanch for a couple of minutes in boiling water. Drain, immediately refresh in cold water and spread the leaves out on a tea towel on the kitchen table.

To make the stuffing: chop, not too finely, the small leaves of the heart, 200 g (7 oz) of veal, 200 g (7 oz) of pork loin, 90 g (3½ oz) of sausagemeat, 1 onion and 3 garlic cloves. Mix well and add 90 g (3½ oz) of grated cheese, 2 whole eggs, 1 cup of Camargue round rice (short-grain rice), salt and pepper. The rice should be uncooked, of course, as its role is to absorb the excess liquid during cooking.

From here on there are two methods, both of which give equally savoury results. The traditional method is for a large stuffed cabbage.

Spread a square of muslin on a table. Place the largest cabbage leaves on top and spread each with a layer of the stuffing. Continue to alternate layers of leaves and stuffing until, little by little, you have re-created the shape of the cabbage.

Wrap the cabbage in the muslin, and tie tightly at the top with a piece of string. In a pot not much larger than the size of the cabbage, place 2 carrots, 1 onion, 2 garlic cloves, a sprig of thyme, a bay leaf and a pinch of salt. Place the cabbage on top and fill the pot with cold water. Cover, place over a medium heat and bring to the boil. Reduce to simmering point and allow to cook for at least 3 hours. Remove the cabbage from the pot, discard the muslin, and serve whole with some of the broth.

The second method is for small cabbages, which around here we affectionately call *paquetouns*. To begin with, make a thin broth by cooking 2 carrots, 1 onion, 2 garlic cloves, a sprig of thyme, a bay leaf, and some salt and pepper, in a pot of water until the vegetables are soft and the broth is well flavoured. Choose the 10 best leaves from the cabbage. Pile on each the remaining less attractive leaves. Place a scoop of stuffing on each pile of leaves, and roll up to form small parcels. Place in a buttered deep baking dish and crown each parcel with a thin slice of streaky bacon. Pour in enough broth to come three-quarters of the way up the cabbage parcels, and cook in a moderate oven for at least 2 hours, adding more broth from time to time as required.

WINE :
Côtes
du Ventoux
rouge

Field Rabbit with
Mustard Sauce
~

WINE :
Gigondas
rouge

This recipe requires a large rabbit cut into pieces, an equal number of strips of streaky bacon, a good Dijon mustard and a lot of thyme. Begin by placing the rabbit in an ovenproof earthenware pot with the thyme, a bay leaf, 4 crushed garlic cloves, a little rosemary (too much will overwhelm the other flavours), and a sliced onion. Add a generous amount of olive oil and then cook slowly for several hours in the oven. Discard the herbs and onion. Brush the rabbit pieces with the Dijon mustard, crown each with a generous sprig of thyme and wrap in a piece of streaky bacon.

Arrange the rabbit pieces in an oiled gratin dish, sprinkle a few breadcrumbs over each piece and cook in a hot oven for a further 30 minutes.

Deglaze the gratin dish with some white wine and 1 teaspoon of wine vinegar, and serve the rabbit piping hot, with baked potatoes and a green salad garnished with garlic croûtons.

Garlic Rabbit
~

WINE :
Côtes
du Luberon
rouge

This recipe requires a flameproof earthenware pot with a lid – the lid must have a small hole in the top to allow steam to escape during cooking. Cut a large rabbit into pieces and brown in olive oil directly in the earthenware pot. When the rabbit is golden, add about 30 unpeeled garlic cloves, a generous handful of chopped parsley and the juice of a large lemon. Season with salt and freshly ground black pepper. Cover the pot and seal the lid with a strip of dough made from flour and water. Cook in a low oven for 2½ hours.

Serve piping hot, with potatoes with bacon (see recipe on page 26), and a green salad.

*Field Rabbit
with Mustard
Sauce*

Baked
Potatoes

~

Before sharing with you some of my favourite potato recipes, I must tell you about the magnificent potatoes from Pertuis. They are as renowned here as Cavaillon melon, Carpentras strawberries and Villelaure artichokes. These potatoes grow in the sandy soil of the Pertuis plains on the banks of the Durance. They are exquisite, best cooked in the oven or pot when new, or otherwise prepared as a mash or gratin.

IN THE KITCHEN : Peel, wash and dry 1.5 kg (3 lb) of good-sized Pertuis potatoes. Cut them into egg-sized pieces. Arrange in a greased baking dish and add half a glass of water, some chopped thyme and a pinch of salt. That's all. Cook them in a moderate oven for 45 minutes.

They should turn golden, slightly swollen and perfectly soft inside. Serve hot with a dab of butter or a sprinkling of good, fruity olive oil.

Potatoes with
Bacon

~

Peel, wash and dry some medium-sized Pertuis potatoes: allow 2 per guest. Cut them into halves, and place a thin slice of streaky bacon across the middle. Tie the halves together with some cooking twine. Cook over a low heat with a small quantity of neutral cooking oil (peanut, for example) in a tightly closed pot for 1 hour. In principle, you should not need to add any salt because of the bacon.

Oraison Gratin

~

Oraison is a beautiful village in Haute-Provence, located on the banks of the Durance between Valensole and Forcalquier. There I have eaten a gratin of potatoes, onion and pork, just perfect after a day's hunting in the woods of Saint-Martin. In the past, it would have been taken to be cooked in the baker's oven, after the bread had been baked. But it will certainly be as good when slowly cooked in your own oven.

In THE KITCHEN : Begin by making a well-flavoured broth using 2 leeks, an onion, a carrot, 2 garlic cloves, a sprig of thyme, a bay leaf, and some salt and pepper in 2 litres (3½ pints) of water.

Place a frying pan over a low heat and brown 2 large onions, sliced, in a mixture of butter and olive oil. Wash, peel and dry 1 kg (2 lb) of old Pertuis potatoes. Slice them finely. In a buttered gratin dish arrange alternate layers of potato slices, onion and grated Gruyère cheese beginning and ending with the potato. Cover with the broth and cook in a hot oven for 30 minutes.

For each guest, take a pork loin chop and coat it in a mixture of pepper, salt and crushed sage leaves. Cover the gratin with the pork chops. Reduce the oven temperature slightly and continue cooking (approximately 45 minutes) until the chops are golden brown.

WINE :
Côtes
de Provence
rouge

Auntie Lilette's
Quince Paste

~

Quinces ripen in October, and this is the time to stock up on quince paste. During my childhood, a piece of quince paste on a slice of bread was our 4 o'clock *goûter* (afternoon tea) for a good part of the year. Alas, despite the significant quantity made each year by Auntie

Lilette, we always managed to run out. For a few days in October, this golden and fragrant paste was set out to dry in all the available dishes, *tians* and salad bowls in the house. They were everywhere – all over the kitchen and the pantry. Once dried, the paste was wrapped in aluminium foil and stacked on the top shelves of the pantry. But the day inevitably came in February when a chocolate bar replaced the fruit paste, and then we had to wait until the following year before enjoying this delicious quince paste once more.

IN THE KITCHEN : Carefully wash 10 or more unblemished quinces. Place them in a pot, cover with water and cook for about 1 hour, or until they are tender and a knife can be inserted easily. Allow to cool, then peel and cut into pieces before mashing in a *moulin à légumes* (vegetable mill). Weigh the resulting pulp, return to the pot and add an equal quantity of sugar. Cook for approximately 30 minutes, stirring constantly with a wooden spoon, to dry and thicken the paste. Be careful not to let the paste catch on the bottom of the pot. Then spoon into dishes and spread to a depth of 2.5 cm (1 inch). Cover with a tea towel and allow to dry for 10 days. Turn the paste over and allow to dry once more. When ready, wrap in aluminium foil, which will allow you to keep it for a long time.

To serve the quince paste, cut it into 2.5 cm (1 inch) squares, and roll them in granulated sugar.

Pear Cake
~

In a large bowl mix 250 g (8 oz) of softened butter with 250 g (8 oz) of caster sugar (flavoured with vanilla). Then beat in 4 large whole eggs, one at a time, and 1 tablespoon of pear liqueur. Add 500 g (1 lb) of plain flour, 2 teaspoons of baking powder and a pinch of salt. Thin the mixture with a little milk if necessary – but it must remain firm enough to support the weight of the fruit. Pour the cake batter into a buttered deep cake tin. Peel 6 or 7 large pears and cut into quarters. Completely cover the cake mixture with the pear pieces and cook in a moderate oven for approximately 50 minutes. You can also make this cake with apples, cherries, blackberries or plums. Whichever fruit you choose the recipe calls for about 2.5 cm (1 inch) of fruit on top of the mixture.

WINE :
Vin cuit
de Salen,
Domaine
des Bastides

Pear Cak
on th
sideboar

Persimmons with Rum

~

This is not really a recipe at all, but for me it's the best way to eat *kakis* – the fruit of the persimmon tree. For a long time, when I was younger, I thought that these beautiful Chinese orange fruit, which suddenly appeared in the autumn as the persimmon tree loses its leaves, were intended to be used as missiles during epic battles after school. Their extremely bitter, unpleasant taste had completely discouraged me from eating them. But I did not know then what I have since learned – that they lose their bitterness with the first frost. They should not be picked before then. If one follows this basic rule and waits until they become very soft and almost translucent, they make a wonderful autumn dessert, cut in half, generously bathed in old rum and sprinkled with sugar.

Persimmon trees

Candied Orange and Lemon Peel

~

This recipe is traditionally made with oranges, but you can also make it with lemons and grapefruit. However, I do advise you to preserve each fruit separately. Choose unblemished and unwaxed fruits with thin skins, wash them, cut them in half and place in a saucepan with a lot of water. Bring to the boil, and simmer for at least 2 hours. The skins should become almost translucent. Drain well and allow to cool. Carefully remove and discard the pulp and seeds, and cut the skins into the longest possible strips approximately 1 cm (½ inch) wide.

At this stage we must pause so that I can tell you how to make *un sirop au filet*. Put 1 kg (2 lb) of sugar cubes in a pan, add 2 tablespoons of glucose and 200 ml (7 fl oz) of water. If you allow the sugar to dissolve over a low heat and then gradually increase the heat, the syrup goes through several stages: *le filet, le soufflé, le boulé, le petit cassé, le grand cassé* and finally *le caramel*.

We are interested in the first stage – *le filet*: once the sugar has dissolved, the syrup is brought to a rolling boil; it starts to thicken and is ready when a drop of it drawn between the thumb and index finger forms a thread. Now add the fruit strips, and cook over a low heat for 1 hour. Drain carefully and allow the candied peel to dry on a cake rack. The following day, roll the peel in caster sugar. Store in an airtight jar.

My Grandmother's Russian Toffee

~

I cherish wonderful memories of a certain tin box, slightly rusty – like the sugar tins you invariably find in the kitchen cupboard – full of thread, buttons, aspirins and Epsom salts, old coins or sugar cubes. My tin had 18th-century dancing marquises surrounded by roses on the lid and it was always filled, as if by a miracle, with small soft cubes wrapped in silver paper. They were the best toffees

on this earth, my Grandmother's Russian toffees. Why Russian, I have no idea, but that's what she called them and the name, which sounded so mysterious and exotic, added to the joy of eating them.

IN THE KITCHEN : In a heavy-bottomed pan, place equal quantities of butter, honey, bitter dark chocolate and caster sugar. Heat slowly, stirring all the time with a wooden spoon. When the mixture reaches boiling point, let it bubble for a couple of minutes, still stirring constantly, until the mixture is smooth and thick. The less you cook it, the softer the toffee. If you continue to cook the toffee, it will be hard – be careful not to let it burn. Carefully pour the contents of the pan on to a buttered baking sheet – a marble slab would be ideal – and let it cool slightly before cutting into squares. I cannot manage to cut out squares as well as my Grandmother. My toffees might not look like much but they taste delicious. Wrap each toffee in aluminium foil and keep them locked away in a metal tin. You are unlikely to be able to keep them for long . . .

Green
Tomato Jam
~

Wash and dry 2 kg (4 lb) of green tomatoes, then cut them up into pieces. Place them in a large copper pan with a large unwaxed lemon, finely sliced, and 1.5 kg (3 lb) of caster sugar. Bring the mixture to the boil, stirring constantly with a wooden spoon, then lower the heat and cook gently for a further 30 minutes. You will have to cook the jam for 30 minutes for three days running. The jam is ready when a blob of the mixture sets when dropped on a plate. While still hot pour the jam into warm, sterilized jars.

You can serve this jam with fresh cheeses like *la brousse du Rove*, see page 165.

WINE :
Côtes
du Rhône
Rasteau
moelleux

andmother's
ssian Toffee

CABBAGE AND ROMANCE

For this chapter, I will be a little indiscreet and tell you how a few years ago I wooed the lady who was shortly afterwards to become my wife. It was our first *tête-à-tête* (intimate dinner) and I decided to make my special cabbage dish. It was November, the days were short and a precocious winter was snapping at our heels. We couldn't possibly have dinner in the kitchen – far too mundane. The dining room was too large, too formal and too boring! I had to find an area which would be both unusual and charming – a wonderful surprise. For a while, I thought of the attic, so romantic and mysterious, but finally I opted for the round-shaped landing on the first floor, with blood-red walls, a floor of terracotta tiles and a green terrazzo skirting board which ran all the way up the

spiral staircase to the attic. I brought up a small round table, to complement the shape of the floor, and two chairs, and I laid the china and cutlery on a pale grey crisp linen tablecloth. I decorated the room with cabbages, beautiful round green cabbages, planted in terracotta pots. I carefully wrapped my present with a light-blue satin bow. I lit the candles and put a few bottles of wine on ice . . . and started to prepare *la potée d'amour*.

y special
bbage dish
the
hâteau de
nge in
mières

Potée d'amour

~

WINE :
Côtes
du Rhône
Rasteau
rouge

As when preparing all magic potions, you need a cauldron – a large metal or earthenware pot – deep and mysterious. To prepare such a dish for two is a bit of an amusing paradox, and rather greedy, but it can easily be turned into a superb meal for twelve. All you need is an even larger earthenware pot and to increase the quantities. I would advise you to add a chicken, which should be cooked on its own in the pot with the wine and water for 1 hour before you add the other ingredients, and a few smoked sausages. But as I am giving it to you, this recipe makes a delicious and very efficient elixir.

IN THE KITCHEN : In the bottom of the pot, place a few thick rashers of streaky bacon, then all the vegetables for the soup (except for the potatoes which are added later): a nice firm head of cabbage that has been blanched for a few minutes in boiling water, 2 carrots, 2 turnips and 2 onions (all peeled and roughly sliced), plus an additional onion studded with cloves. On top of the vegetables, place the meats: a small pork shank, some spare-ribs, a piece of smoked streaky bacon, and 2 garlic sausages, pierced with a fork to prevent them from bursting. Then, in the middle of all that, a large pippin apple. You will also need 3 pieces of star anise, a bay leaf, some freshly ground black pepper and a little salt (not too much, because of the salted meats). Pour 2 large glasses of a good dry white wine into the pot and add enough water to cover the meats. Put the lid on the pot and gently simmer for 1 hour. Then add 2 potatoes and a small piece of ham. Simmer for a further hour.
Serve piping hot with pickled gherkins and mustards, but without the broth.

Pot-au-feu

~

This dish is not really suitable for two – it is an abundant convivial dish ideal for sharing with a large gathering of friends around a sizeable table. In most cuisines around the world similar versions of this recipe can be found. And, of course, there is a traditional Provençal version in which three different kinds of meat are used: beef, lamb and pork.

In the kitchen : From the butcher, you will need to buy 1 kg (2 lb) of beef, a shoulder of lamb (or a few lamb shanks) and as many smoked sausages as there are guests. Don't forget a marrow bone. When I have a lot of guests, I always add a veal shank and a chicken, as in the previous recipe. Put all the meats, except for the sausages and the bone, in a large pot and cover them with unsalted cold water. Place the pan over a low heat and bring the water slowly to the boil; carefully skim the surface several times. Lower the heat to maintain a very slow boil and then add a large onion studded with cloves, a few unpeeled garlic cloves, a bouquet garni (made with some parsley, a bay leaf, a sprig of thyme, some chervil, the green of a leek and a celery stalk, tied together with a small piece of string), a nice piece of dried melon skin, some coarse sea salt, and a few peppercorns. I normally add 2 or 3 sugar lumps.

Let the pot-au-feu cook gently for at least 3 hours. You can then add the white part of a few leeks tied in a bunch, some carrots, turnips, a slice of pumpkin, the marrow bone (tied in a muslin bag so that the marrow doesn't dissolve into the stock), and finally the sausages, pricked with a fork. Cook for a further hour.

While the broth is still simmering skim off all the fat with a flat spoon.

Serve the broth separately, in warmed bowls. If it looks too pale, you can improve the colour by adding 1–2 table-spoons of caramel (see recipe on page 41). Spread the meats and vegetables in a large warmed serving dish with some potatoes (that have been cooked separately in their skins). Serve your pot-au-feu piping hot with pickles, mustards, coarse sea salt and a bowl of *sauce rouge* and *sauce verte* (see recipes on page 38).

Wine: Côtes du Rhône Villages rouge

Sauce Rouge and Sauce Verte

~

Sauce rouge is a simple tomato *coulis* with a touch of cayenne pepper (see recipe on page 159).

Sauce verte is my friend Bruno's recipe. First, he chops up a big bunch of parsley and a garlic clove. Then, in a pan over a low heat, he cooks the parsley and garlic with 1 tablespoon of butter and 1 tablespoon of olive oil for a couple of minutes. He adds 1 tablespoon of breadcrumbs and stirs constantly with a wooden spoon until slightly brown. Then Bruno adds a dash of wine vinegar and a pinch of salt and sugar. When the sauce has cooled, all you have to do is thin it down with a little olive oil and serve.

Catherine's Roast Pork with Sage

~

Not long after we were married, I banished Catherine from the kitchen. She didn't mind at all and all her friends seemed to be extremely envious. However, I would like to point out that Catherine is a wonderful cook, as you will discover from this recipe for roast pork with garlic and sage, on a bed of potatoes *à la boulangère*. Choose a large loin of pork, as it tends to shrink a little when cooked.

Anyway, if there is any left over, cold roast pork is delicious.

Put the loin in the middle of a large earthenware dish. Peel several cloves of garlic, cut them in half or quarter them if they are too large, make several deep incisions in the meat and insert a piece of garlic into each incision. Baste the joint with a little peanut oil and rub with some fresh sage leaves, and some sprigs of thyme. Season generously with coarse sea salt and freshly ground black pepper. Add a few dabs of butter and some bay leaves and place the dish in a medium to slow oven; the roast should be cooked slowly – about 2 hours for a 1.5 kg (3 lb) loin. If it starts to brown too much, add a few drops of water to the dish and lower the heat, but if the oven is slow enough you should not have to do that.

An hour before the roast is cooked, place some peeled potatoes – cut in half or quartered if they are large – around the meat. Put the roast back into the oven. Turn the meat two or three times during cooking, as well as the potatoes, to ensure they brown evenly. When ready, the potatoes should be nicely golden and crisp on the outside and meltingly tender inside.

WINE:
Côtes
de Provence
rouge

Small Salads

~

After *pot-au-feu* or *potée d'amour*, you can't eat much more than a salad – like this delicious and refreshing salad of carrots, courgettes and spinach.

Choose very fresh, young and tender vegetables. Remove and discard the stalks from the spinach, and carefully wash and dry the leaves. Peel the carrots and the courgettes and, using a vegetable peeler, cut them lengthways into fine strips. Mix these strips with the spinach leaves and dress them with a simple vinaigrette made with olive oil, salt, pepper and lemon juice. Alternatively serve a nice Banon goats' cheese preserved in olive oil (see page 40) on a bed of lamb's lettuce scattered with a few crushed hazelnuts, or just a simple plain green salad (see page 96).

A Jar of
Goats' Cheese
in Olive Oil

~

WINE :
Côtes
du Luberon
blanc

If you go to Banon, do not forget to buy a supply of their famous little goats' cheeses. Buy them fairly dry, so you will be able to preserve them easily in olive oil. Choose a large sterilized glass jar with a lid. At the bottom, put a layer of these little cheeses and ideally sprinkle them with *sarriette*, a herb we call *pèbre d'âse* around here. *Sarriette* will flavour the oil and the cheeses and it's unnecessary to add any other herbs. You are not making a *bouillabaisse*! Fill the jar with alternate layers of cheeses and *sarriette*. Cover with a good olive oil, seal the jar and marinate for a month before using.

Sarriette grows wild in southern Europe and tastes like a cross between mint and thyme – thyme could be used instead.

My Cousin Jeanne's
Saint-Honoré

~

Saint-Honoré is a marvellous cake made up of puffs of choux pastry, filled with *crème pâtissière*, stuck together with caramel on a pastry base and covered with chantilly cream. Caramel, which gives its deep colour to meat stock, its delicate flavour to creams and its brittle texture to countless desserts, is easy to make, if a little tricky. In fact, caramel is the stage sugar reaches just before it burns.

IN THE KITCHEN : You will need a saucepan, about 20 sugar lumps and a few drops of water – about 1 tablespoon. Place the saucepan, containing the sugar and water, over a medium heat. First the sugar will dissolve, then start foaming. At that point you will need to concentrate – watch your pan carefully – everything is going to happen very quickly. Suddenly, at the heart of the boiling syrup, there will be a brown spot which will spread rapidly and become darker, smoking a little. Immediately remove the saucepan from the heat and shake it gently to produce an even-coloured brown syrup. This is a crucial moment – if you wait just a few seconds longer, the syrup will burn! But if you stop the heat on time, it will take on a lovely colour. Too light, it will be tasteless, too dark, it will be bitter. Use it straight away while it's still liquid because it hardens very quickly as it cools down. If you want to flavour a custard or colour a broth you can also dilute the caramel with a drop of water, which will soften it, but this would be entirely useless for our *Saint-Honoré*.

Let us go back to the beginning of the recipe for the *Saint-Honoré*. To make the shortcrust pastry, rub 125 g (4 oz) of butter into 250 g (8 oz) of flour, add a pinch of salt and mix with 1 egg and 1–2 tablespoons of water to form a soft dough. Let the pastry rest for 1–2 hours. Roll the pastry out to form a 5 mm (¼ inch) thick circle, using a plate to cut out the shape. Carefully transfer the pastry to a buttered and floured baking sheet, prick it with a fork and place it in a moderate oven to cook for a good 20 minutes.

Make the choux pastry. In a saucepan, bring to the boil 500 ml (17 fl oz) of water, 200 g (7 oz) of butter, 15 g (½ oz) of salt and 30 g (1¼ oz) of caster sugar. As soon as the mixture starts boiling, add 400 g (13 oz) of plain flour – all at once. Take the pan off the heat and beat the dough with a wooden spoon until it stops sticking to the sides of the pan. Let it cool a little, then gradually add 12 eggs, beating well between each one. Place the dough in a piping bag and pipe blobs of dough on to buttered baking sheets. Make sure you leave enough space between each blob because they are going to puff up and triple in volume. Cook for about 25 minutes in a moderately hot oven.

Then make the *crème pâtissière*. In a bowl, mix 250 g (8 oz) of caster sugar, 60 g (2½ oz) of plain flour, 6 egg yolks and a pinch of salt. Bring 500 ml (17 fl oz) of milk to the boil and then gradually add it to the egg mixture, beating constantly with a whisk. Pour the contents of the bowl into a saucepan, bring back to the boil, stirring constantly with a wooden spoon, and cook for a few minutes until the mixture is thick and smooth. Keep stirring the cream until it is cold to avoid a skin forming, which would make it lumpy.

Now make some golden brown caramel (see previous page). Fill each choux puff with *crème pâtissière* and then dip into the caramel. Stick the choux puffs around the edge of the shortcrust pastry base so they fit close together, and drizzle more caramel over each one. Then carefully pour the remaining *crème pâtissière* on to the pastry round, in the middle of the ring of choux puffs.

The cake is traditionally decorated by piping on rosettes of chantilly cream (see recipe on page 196). The top is then decorated with more caramelized choux puffs filled with *crème pâtissière*. But for our *tête-à-tête* I chose to cover the cake with a thick layer of chantilly cream, then I placed the cake on a bed of crystallized mint leaves. On top, I drew a large heart of sugar rose petals, made according to the following recipe.

Sugar Flowers

~

Nasturtium flowers, violets, acacia and orange blossoms, mint leaves or rose petals are all perfect for this recipe.

Pick the blooms or the leaves from your garden on the same day you will be using them, ideally just before preparing them.

For the rose petals, choose unblemished red, old-fashioned velvety roses, which are softer and more perfumed than most modern hybrid roses. Be careful not to bruise the petals.

Beat 2 egg whites until just stiff. Use tweezers to dip the petals and leaves one by one into the egg whites, then into icing sugar. Carefully lay them on a clean baking sheet. Put them in a very slow oven, and cook them the same way you would for meringues, but leaving the oven door slightly ajar. The idea is to dry the flowers, not to cook them. Let them cool on a wire rack.

If you are not going to use your sugar flowers or leaves straight away, they should be stored in an airtight tin.

*My Cous
Jeann
Saint-Honor
decorated wi
sugar flowe*

TEATIME IN THE KITCHEN

In December, in the clear light of a winter's day, the Luberon becomes a magnificent array of greys, blues and yellows. If you go for a brisk walk in the afternoon you can work up a warming glow, but as soon as the sun dips down behind the hills, you have to retreat back home.

On your return, having hung the coats and scarves in the hallway, and having run across the freezing corridors of this old barn of a house – too difficult to heat – you can take refuge in the kitchen, warmed by a bright burning fire and smelling exquisitely of sugar, butter and vanilla. With rosy cheeks and eyes bright with expectation, everyone is ready for a delicious afternoon tea. On the long wooden table covered with a linen cloth are bowls and cups, a large pot of dark, thick, steamy hot chocolate, a jug of warm milk, a slab of sweet butter, some delicious slices of country bread, a selection of cheeses and jams, a splendid fruit cake gleaming with candied fruit or studded with sultanas, a huge apple and caramel cake and a chocolate cake, together with spice cake smelling of aniseed and a basket of miniature vanilla crescents . . .

Chocolate Cake, Caramel and Apple Cake, and Little Vanilla Crescents

Pages 46–47: The kitchen at the Château d'Ansouis

45

Hot Chocolate

~

This is very simple but very rewarding and warming on a cold winter's day. Bring 1 litre (1¾ pints) of fresh milk slowly to the boil and add 150 g (5 oz) of good quality dark bitter chocolate. Place the pan back over a very low heat and simmer for a few minutes to allow the chocolate to melt, stirring constantly with a whisk. Serve piping hot.

Fruit Cake

~

The best fruits on this earth are grown in the river valleys of the Rhône and the Durance. They are lined with strawberry and melon fields, cherry trees, peach trees, apricot trees, plum and pear trees, which are protected from the mistral winds by fences and tall cypress trees. So, naturally, not far from those fields and orchards, around Apt and Aix, people have long learnt to master the art of crystallizing fruit. In St Rémy-de-Provence, for instance, there is an old factory where the floors are sticky with sugar and the kitchens filled with the vapours coming from boiling copper pans. The dark vaulted rooms are piled up with large earthenware vessels overflowing with glacé cherries, peaches, plums, angelica and apricots. In another room, the fruits are carefully encased in lace doilies and placed in little wooden crates before being sent to the four corners of the world. You feel as though you have discovered Snow White and the Seven Dwarves' jewel mine.

As a matter of fact, it is with these fruit jewels that we decorate the crown for the king on Twelfth Night: angelica for the emeralds and cherries for the rubies.

Fruit Cake and Sultana Cake

IN THE KITCHEN : Let us go back to our *goûter* (afternoon tea). Here is the fruit cake recipe.

The day before, soak 125 g (4 oz) of mixed glacé fruit (mixed peel, melon, peach and apricot) chopped, 125 g (4 oz) of whole glacé cherries and 125 g (4 oz) of golden sultanas in as much old rum as you need to cover the fruit.

The following day beat together 125 g (4 oz) of butter with 125 g (4 oz) of caster sugar and a pinch of salt until the mixture is smooth and pale. Then little by little add 3 eggs, beating well after each addition. Add the grated zest of a large unwaxed lemon followed by 250 g (8 oz) of plain flour and 1 teaspoon of baking powder. Strain the fruit and add them to the cake mixture with 1 tablespoon of the soaking rum (keep the rest in a bottle or a jar – you will be able to use it for your next cake).

Butter a loaf tin or cake tin, line it with greaseproof paper, then pour in the batter, allowing space for it to almost double in size during cooking. Bake in a moderate oven for 45 minutes (the cake is cooked when a skewer or the blade of a knife is inserted into the centre and comes out clean). Take the cake out of the oven, turn it out of the tin and let it cool on a wire rack. Then wrap it up in aluminium foil and wait at least 24 hours before eating. I promise you your patience will be amply rewarded!

Every year, in January, I make a different version of this cake with the leftovers of the Christmas 13 'desserts' (see recipe on page 70). Proceed according to the above recipe but replace the candied fruit and the sultanas with dried figs, tailed and chopped up, and pitted dates soaked in rum. You can also add chopped walnuts, almonds and hazelnuts, pieces of dark nougat, almond paste and quince paste.

Sultana Cake

~

Beat together 200 g (7 oz) of softened butter with 200 g (7 oz) of caster sugar, 1 tablespoon of vanilla sugar and a pinch of salt until pale, smooth and creamy. Add 4 whole eggs, one at a time, then 500 g (1 lb) of plain flour and 2 teaspoons of baking powder. Add 125 ml (4 fl oz) of rum, 150 g (5 oz) of currants and 150 g (5 oz) of sultanas and mix well. Pour the batter into a buttered loaf tin or cake tin lined with grease-proof paper.

Bake in a moderate oven for approximately 45 minutes.

Once cooked turn the cake out and let it cool on a rack.

Simple Apple Tart

~

First, make the pastry by mixing 250 g (8 oz) of plain flour with 125 g (4 oz) of caster sugar, a pinch of salt, and 2 teaspoons of vanilla sugar. Rub in 150 g (5 oz) of softened butter until the mixture resembles fine breadcrumbs and bind with 1 whole egg. Lightly knead, then allow the pastry to rest for at least 30 minutes in a cool place.

In another bowl, beat 150 g (5 oz) of softened butter with 125 g (4 oz) of caster sugar until pale, then add 1 whole egg. When the mixture is smooth, gently fold in 100 g (3½ oz) of plain flour. Whip 250 ml (8 fl oz) of double cream until stiff and lightly fold it into the butter mixture. Roll out the pastry and use to line a buttered and floured tart tin. Peel and core 5 large apples, slice them (not too finely) and arrange them on the pastry case. Carefully pour the batter over the fruit.

Finally sprinkle a few slivered almonds and a little caster sugar over the top of the tart. Bake in a moderate oven for no longer than 1 hour. Allow the tart to cool before serving.

Wine:
Muscat
de Beaumes
de Venise,
served chilled

Caramel and Apple Cake

~

In a large bowl beat 4 whole eggs with 200 g (7 oz) of caster sugar and 2 teaspoons of vanilla sugar. Stir in 150 g (5 oz) of melted butter, then gradually add 200 g (7 oz) of flour and 2 teaspoons of baking powder.

Make a golden caramel (see recipe on page 41) and pour it into a fairly deep cake tin. Peel, core and quarter 4 or 5 large apples. Arrange them as closely as possible on the caramel, round side down, and pour the batter over them. Bake in a moderate oven for a good half hour. Turn the cake out on to the serving plate as soon as it is cooked and before the caramel has had time to harden.

If you make this cake the day before and wrap it in foil when it is cold, it will taste even better.

Chocolate Cake

~

Make a syrup with 150 g (5 oz) of granulated sugar and 1 tablespoon of water. When it starts foaming, turn the heat down and stir in 300 g (10 oz) of bitter chocolate. Off the heat, stir in 250 g (8 oz) of butter, 3 eggs (one at a time), and 80 g (3¼ oz) of sifted flour. Pour the cake batter into a deep, buttered cake tin, and bake in a bain-marie for about 1 hour in a moderate oven, 180°C (350°F), Gas Mark 4.

When cooked, turn out the cake directly on to the serving plate because it should not be handled too much. Once it has cooled down completely carefully cover it with a piece of aluminium foil.

The most difficult part is yet to come! You absolutely must hide it in a cool place, but not in the refrigerator, for at least 24 hours, and resist the temptation to serve it straight away. Another piece of advice. If you have a problem turning the cake out of the tin, which happens sometimes, do not worry: smooth out the top with the blade of a knife and sprinkle it with icing sugar or powdered cocoa, and nobody will be the wiser.

Honey Spice Cake

~

Provence has always produced many kinds of honey – the most famous of all, lavender honey, is far from being my favourite – its strong flavour lacks delicacy. It is such a pity that the great beauty of lavender fields does not transfer itself to the honey! I prefer *garrigue* honey, in which the perfumes of lavender, thyme and all the other flowers of the hills are blended. It is perfect for black nougat (see recipe on page 68), in honey spice cake, or simply spread on a slice of bread. I should also mention acacia honey, light and very delicately perfumed.

IN THE KITCHEN : In a large bowl, mix together 250 g (8 oz) of plain flour, 125 g (4 oz) of caster sugar, 1 teaspoon of bicarbonate of soda, 1 teaspoon of mixed spice, 2 teaspoons of aniseed, ½ teaspoon of ground cinnamon and ½ teaspoon of ground cloves. Add 2 teaspoons of rum and 2 tablespoons of honey to 250 ml (8 fl oz) of boiled milk. Little by little pour the liquid on to the dry ingredients. Stir with a spoon until the batter is smooth. Cover and stand overnight at room temperature.
The next day spoon the batter into a greased and base-lined 500 g (1 lb) loaf tin; it should not be more than half full. Cover with foil and bake in a preheated oven, 180°F (350°C), Gas Mark 4, for 45 minutes. Turn the cake out on to a wire rack and allow it to cool completely.

Orange Cake

~

For this recipe you need: 125 g (4 oz) of caster sugar, 200 g (7 oz) of plain flour, 2 teaspoons of baking powder, the grated rind of 1 orange and 1 lemon, the juice of the orange, 50 g (2 oz) of candied orange peel (finely chopped), 125 g (4 oz) of butter and 3 egg yolks.
In a bowl, mix together the sugar, the flour and the baking powder. Add the grated rinds, the orange juice and the peel, then stir in the softened butter and the egg yolks. Choose a large shallow tin (for instance a flan tin) so the cake will not be too thick. Butter the tin generously and spoon in the cake batter. Cook for no more than an hour in a medium to hot oven. It is delicious eaten when still warm, so serve it straight away.

Rose-hip Jam

~

To start with, around October, you will need to find a wild rose bush. You know, the dog rose or the briar type, with plump, bright red fruit, which learned people call *cynorhodons*. You will need a basketful of these. Back home, remove the hips that are too dry. Keep them for making rose-hip tea when you have a cold, as they are very high in vitamin C. With the ripe hips, we are going to make a delicious jam. First, you need to remove the seeds. Split the fruit lengthways, as if you were stoning a date, and scrape out the seeds and any 'hairy bits'. These 'hairy bits' used to be sold as itching powder in joke shops, which is why in Provence, where we call a cat a cat, we have nicknamed these 'ass-scratchers'. But let us go back to our jam. Once you have cleaned the rose-hips, weigh them and put them in a preserving pan with 750 g (1½ lb) of granulated sugar per kilo (2 lb) of fruit. Cover and leave to macerate overnight. The following day, cook the fruit and sugar for 30 minutes. You will have to cook the jam for 30 minutes on three successive days. Then pour the jam into sterilized jars.

Serve this jam for tea with large slices of buttered country bread.

Bitter Orange Marmalade

~

We make bitter orange marmalade a little late, in January or February, when the fruit is ripe and when, after a trip to the Côte d'Azur, we drive back, the car filled with blooming mimosa to decorate the house and with baskets of bitter oranges.

In the kitchen : First place 1 kg (2 lb) of apples, quartered but not peeled or cored, in a large pan with 1 litre (1¾ pints) of water. Cover and cook over a low heat for about an hour, stirring occasionally to make sure the apples are not burning. When the apples are cooked,

The copper preserving pan

collect all the liquid by letting the apples drip through a fine sieve into a bowl. Meanwhile, carefully peel off the rind of 10 bitter oranges, 10 sweet oranges and 1 unwaxed lemon. Make sure you do not take any pith with the rind. Cut the rind into thin strips and place in a pan of boiling water, then simmer over a low heat until they are translucent and tender. This will take about 20 minutes. Drain the rind, and discard the liquid.

In a copper pan, mix 1 litre (1¾ pints) of the apple juice with 2 litres (3½ pints) of orange juice (half bitter orange and half sweet orange juice). Add the juice of the lemon, the cooked rinds, and 3 kg (6 lb) of granulated sugar. Bring to a rolling boil and after a few minutes, turn off the heat and let the marmalade cool. It can easily boil over so do watch the marmalade constantly when it is boiling. Repeat this operation the following day. Then again the day after that. Then you can pour the marmalade into sterilized jars.

Like the rose-hip jam, this marmalade is perfect on buttered bread.

Little Vanilla
Crescents
~

Put 210 g (7¼ oz) of butter, 210 g (7¼ oz) of plain flour, 100 g (3½ oz) of ground almonds and 50 g (2 oz) of caster sugar into a large bowl and mix together with your fingers until a dough forms. Let the dough rest in the refrigerator for an hour. Then form it into little moon-shaped biscuits the size of a mandarin segment. Arrange them on a buttered baking sheet, leaving room for spreading. Cook in a moderate oven for about 20 minutes but watch them constantly because they must remain pale, and not brown at all. Take them out of the oven and, while they are still hot, roll them in a mixture of caster sugar and vanilla sugar. You must be very careful doing this because these biscuits can crumble easily when they are still hot from the oven. Let the biscuits cool before eating them. I have not mentioned storing them in a tin, because it is virtually impossible to resist eating them all straight away.

Bread an
butter wit
rose-hip jar

A Christmas Supper in Provence

Christmas celebrations start here on the 4th December, Saint Barbe's Day. On that day, we go and gather some fresh moss from the hills. We then put the moss in little saucers and sprinkle over some wheat kernels or lentils with a few drops of water. During the twenty days to Christmas, the wheat or lentils will sprout into lovely green tufts, symbols of life lying dormant during the winter months, representing the harvest to come. This greenery will find its place among the rocks and the bushes of the Christmas crib. The most beautiful one will be kept to decorate the Christmas table.

Every year, a few days before the hallowed evening, we go and find the two cardboard boxes put away the year before at the back of the wardrobe, which hold the clay *santons* (ornamental figures for the Christmas crib) wrapped in cotton wool. The day we set up the Christmas crib, we leave early in the morning with a large basket, to gather moss to make the fields, sprigs of thyme to represent the olive trees, little twigs of cedar for the pine trees and some stones of different sizes for the rocks. These can also be made with paper, thick grey paper that you colour with brown and yellow and red ochre. We used to be able to buy it ready made at the corner shop; we called it crib paper. We also use foil to make up the river where we put the angler and the washerwoman. A small piece of mirror will do for the pond where the ducks will swim. Back home, we spread all of these on a large piece of cardboard which is placed on the sideboard. Then we take the figurines out of their boxes and find them a place in this lovely landscape. The Christmas crib is now ready but only at midnight will the infant Jesus be placed on his bed of straw between the ox and the donkey. For the people of Provence, Christmas is, of course, a religious feast, but it is also the celebration of the land of Provence, because these little figures in their traditional costumes have, for generations, transplanted the mystery of Bethlehem somewhere between Mount Ventoux and Marseilles harbour.

But let us go back to our Christmas supper, a meal which is both frugal and abundant. The table will be set with three white tablecloths, three candles and the saucer containing moss and sprouting wheat. There will be no meat. First, the bread, a large loaf marked with a cross, then the *aïgo boulido* (a soup whose name literally means boiled water), celery with anchovies, the *tian* of cardoons, a dish of fresh fish from the coast, eel from the Rhône river banks or salt cod from St Malo. Then will come the goats' cheeses served with a curly endive salad 'just like baby Jesus' hair' and, of course, the famous 13 desserts (traditionally dried fruits and nuts).

I must also mention the log. Not the cake with buttercream, which we will talk about tomorrow. I mean the real log, the one celebrated in the ceremony of *cacho-fio*, taken from a dead fruit tree, usually an almond tree. On this night it is blessed with a little hot wine by the head of the family, then offered to the fire by the youngest member of the family. This ceremony symbolizes the eternity of life. In fact, in Provence, Christmas is the celebration of life – the life of the new-born child, of the wheat germinating and ripening. So mistletoe is not part of the Christmas decor, because it is a cruel parasite, attractive, but sooner or later causing the death of the tree on which it grows. Never give mistletoe to a Provençal; he would be a little offended and would decline – 'No, my trees are fine, thank you'. No mistletoe and, in principle, no Christmas tree either. But being half Alsatian, at home we always had, and we still have, a Christmas tree.

'L'Aïgo Boulido'

~

'Boiled water' is the simplest soup in the world. In Provence, they say *l'aïgo boulido sauvo la vido* (boiled water is a life-saver) and as a matter of fact, this soup accomplishes miracles after a heavy meal or when you have the flu. But then they also add, with a touch of irony and a good deal of philosophy, *'au bout d'un tems, tuo li gènt'* (after a while, it kills people), which means you cannot live on boiled water alone. Anyway, it is absolutely delicious and is the traditional first course of the Christmas supper.

IN THE KITCHEN : You need 3 or 4 garlic cloves per person. Do not peel them, but crush them slightly. Boil the garlic for about 10 minutes in salted water. Then turn off the heat, add a little thyme, a bay leaf and a lot of sage. Cover the pan and let the herbs infuse. Then strain the soup into a clean pan and heat it again without letting it boil. Serve it in a tureen; each soup plate should contain a slice of toasted bread moistened with a little olive oil and covered with thin slices of Gruyère cheese, which will melt in the hot soup.

Celery with Anchovies

~

At the market, choose a large bunch of white celery. Wash and dry it and discard all the blemished parts. Cut the tender stalks and the white leaves into small pieces.

Take 6 or 7 salted anchovies, fillet them and then wash under cold running water. Pat the fillets dry and then mash with a fork. Place the fillets in a frying pan with 1 small glass of olive oil, 1 tablespoon of vinegar and some freshly ground pepper.

No garlic is used in this sauce because it would alter the flavour of the anchovies. Cook this mixture over a low heat – the anchovies must dissolve in the oil without ever boiling. This will take approximately 15 minutes and you need to stir the mixture constantly. Use a heat diffuser under the frying pan if necessary. Stir the celery into the warm anchovy sauce and serve immediately.

Spinach and Pine Nut Tart

~

At this time of year, the greens used are normally either Swiss chard or spinach leaves. Both are delicious. You can even use a combination of the two. Whichever you choose, wash the leaves and blanch them in boiling water for 5 minutes. Drain them and squeeze all the liquid out of the leaves.

Make a shortcrust pastry with 250 g (8 oz) of flour, a pinch of salt, 50 g (2 oz) of butter, 3 tablespoons of olive oil and 3 tablespoons of water. Roll out the pastry and line a tart tin, prick the base with a fork and bake blind in a moderate oven for 15 minutes. It should not brown.

Meanwhile, in a bowl, mix 2 egg yolks, 150 ml (¼ pint) of thick cream and 100 g (3½ oz) of grated Gruyère cheese; season with a pinch of salt and a little freshly ground pepper.

Take the pastry out of the oven. Arrange the blanched green leaves in the pastry case, then pour the cream mixture over them. Sprinkle with 100 g (3½ oz) of pine nuts, decorate with a few black olives and then put the tart back in the oven for a further 20 minutes.

Serve it hot or warm, after the *aïgo boulido*, accompanied by the celery with anchovies.

Cardoon Tian

~

Choose a bunch of white cardoons. To peel them, wear plastic gloves or your hands will be stained for quite a while – that is the one problem with this delicious vegetable. So, peel the stalks and remove all the stringy parts. Cut them up into 5 cm (2 inch) pieces. To prevent them darkening soak them in a bowl of water to which lemon juice has been added. Meanwhile add a handful of flour to a large pan

filled with water, bring it to the boil and add the cardoons. Cook for about 1 hour. When the cardoons are nice and tender, drain them. Place the cardoons in a heavy-bottomed pan with 3 tablespoons of olive oil, 1 onion, 2 garlic cloves, coarsely chopped, and 2 anchovy fillets. Cook for a few minutes over a very low heat. Then sprinkle the cardoons with 50 g (2 oz) of flour, mix well and cook, stirring, for

Spinach and Pine Nut Tart, and Celery with Anchovies

1–2 minutes. Pour over 500 ml (17 fl oz) of hot milk, and stir constantly until the sauce thickens. Season with some sea salt and freshly ground pepper, and then transfer the mixture to a *tian* or baking dish. Cover with some grated Gruyère cheese and brown in a hot oven for 15 minutes.

Now I am going to give you another recipe, not as traditional maybe, but just as delicious and which does not overpower the delicate flavour of the cardoons.

When the cardoons are cooked and very tender, drain them and put them in a baking dish.

Make a white sauce with 50 g (2 oz) of butter, 50 g (2 oz) of flour and 500 ml (17 fl oz) of milk. Add salt and freshly ground pepper to taste. When cooked, add 6 tablespoons of single cream and 60 g (2½ oz) of grated Gruyère cheese. Pour the sauce over the cardoons and sprinkle with additional grated cheese. Brown in a hot oven for 15 minutes.

Truffle Stew

~

I know, you are going to tell me that this dish is far too expensive and too extravagant for Christmas supper – even when you can buy the truffles at the Carpentras market where they are a lot cheaper than in Paris. But what a wonderful dish! In December, truffles are in full season, and there was a time when, in Vaucluse, truffles were as common as potatoes. They were used in beef stew the way carrots are now. So, on Christmas Eve, after the celery and the cardoon, I always serve this delicious truffle stew.

IN THE KITCHEN : You need at least 1 kg (2 lb) of truffles. That's right! Brush them carefully, peel them and

reserve the peelings for the creamed cod dish we are going to make later on.

WINE : Châteauneuf-du-Pape blanc

Truffles from Carpentras

Brown a chopped shallot in a mixture of butter and olive oil. Brown it lightly – do not allow it to burn. Add half a bottle of white Châteauneuf-du-Pape and cook over a low heat until two-thirds of the liquid has evaporated. Season with sea salt and freshly ground pepper and add the truffles cut in 5 mm (¼ inch) thick slices. Stir, then cover and cook for 3 or 4 minutes, only until the stew is hot enough for the truffles to release their flavour. Serve immediately.

Salt Cod with Leeks

~

Some people might wonder why salt cod, caught in the faraway northern seas and salted by fishermen in St Malo, has become so common in Provence that it features in the Christmas supper. It is because the fishermen of St Malo needed huge quantities of salt to preserve their fish, and they found it in abundance on the shores of the Mediterranean and more specifically on the salt flats near the Rhône delta. This is why they exchanged salt cod for salt. The fish, which kept beautifully despite the hot weather, met with considerable success.

IN THE KITCHEN : The day before, soak 1 kg (2 lb) of salt cod in water to wash the salt away. Change the water several times while the fish is soaking. The following day, poach the cod in unsalted water; the water should be 'trembling', but should never actually boil. Take 3 kg (6 lb) of large white leeks. Peel and discard the outer leaves, then wash the leeks carefully. Cut them into 2.5 cm (1 inch) pieces, and cook in boiling water

Cardoons and salt cod

WINE: Côtes de Provence rosé

for 5 minutes. Drain the leeks. Put 3 tablespoons of olive oil, a garlic clove and a small onion, finely chopped, into a heavy-bottomed pan over a low heat. Add the leeks, cover and leave them to cook until very tender. This will take about 20 minutes. Then add a bowl of black olives and the cod, skinned, boned and flaked. Mix with the leeks. Add a few tablespoons of the cod cooking water, half-cover the pan, and allow the mixture to simmer for about 1 hour, over a very low heat. Before serving, taste to check the seasoning; grind some pepper fresh from the pepper mill into the salt cod mixture.

Creamed Salt Cod Tian
~

I ate this for the first time many years ago in St Tropez and since then it has always been a part of our family Christmas menu.

The day before, soak about 1 kg (2 lb) of salt cod in water to wash away the salt. You will need to change the water several times when soaking.

Poach the cod in unsalted water, without letting the water boil. Allow the fish to cool completely, then carefully remove and discard the skin and bones. Flake the flesh and reserve the nicest pieces – about half of the cod. In a food processor purée the rest of the fish with a garlic clove, 1 cup of good olive oil and the truffle peel, if you have made the truffle stew (see page 65). If you are feeling really virtuous and are a stickler for tradition, you could cream the mixture using a pestle and mortar.

In another pan, cook 1 kg (2 lb) of old Pertuis potatoes, peeled, in lightly salted water. When they are cooked, purée them with a masher or in a vegetable mill. Do not use a blender, or you would end up with potato glue. Add enough hot milk (but not too much) to make a fairly light mixture. Carefully fold the puréed cod into the potato with 4 tablespoons of double cream, the reserved flakes of cod and 2 beaten eggs. Season with freshly ground pepper and sea salt, if necessary. Pour the mixture into a gratin dish. Sprinkle some grated cheese and a few black olives over the top. Drizzle a little olive oil over the gratin and allow it to brown in a moderate oven for 30 minutes.

WINE: Côtes de Provence rosé

Orange Butter Fougasse

~

We call it that because it is a *fougasse* recipe from Orange and not because it has anything to do with the fruit of the same name. *Fougasse* is a flat bread from the south of France; it is often flavoured with olives or herbs. Everywhere else it is made with olive oil but in Orange it is made with butter. At the bakers, buy the equivalent of a baguette of raw bread dough. Work it by hand with 75 g (3 oz) of softened butter until the butter has been completely absorbed by the dough. Flatten the dough with your hands and shape it to form an oval about 1 cm (½ inch) thick. Make slits in the dough with a knife as if you were drawing the veins of a leaf. Then put the *fougasse* on a buttered and floured baking sheet. Make sure you open up the slits. Let it

Christmas breakfast

rise for 1 hour, then cook it in a moderate oven for a good 15 minutes. To serve it you must never cut it with a knife, just break it with your hands, like the bread at the Last Supper.

Black Nougat

~

White nougat is a confection that requires technical expertise, but black nougat can be made easily at home. Buy a sheet of *pain azyme* (rice paper), 1 kg (2 lb) of set honey and 500 g (1 lb) of whole almonds, still in their brown skins. Melt

the honey in a pan, add the almonds and cook for about 40 minutes, stirring constantly with a wooden spoon. The nougat is cooked when a drop of the honey mixture solidifies when dropped in a glass of cold water. Take the pan off the heat and let the mixture cool a bit, still stirring. If the nougat is too hot, it will melt the rice paper. Put half of the rice paper on a marble slab. Make a border with metal rulers, like the ones teachers used to punish naughty pupils with. Pour the nougat inside the border on the rice paper, then put the second half of the rice paper on top of it. Take a small breadboard and press lightly on the nougat to make it more compact. After 30 minutes, you can cut it into strips 5–6 cm (about 2 inches) long.

Calissons

This marvellous confection from Aix-en-Provence was created a long time ago as a result of a love affair between a pastry chef and his queen. The legend says that the good King René used to go hunting often – too often for his beautiful wife. Queen Jeanne, tired of waiting for him, became very friendly with her young and dashing pastry chef. The chef, madly in love with his royal mistress, invented a little sweetmeat to please her – the *calisson*. Traditionally *calissons* are made with a mixture of almonds and candied melon. In this recipe, I have replaced the melon with orange peel as I prefer it.

IN THE KITCHEN : You need the same weight of almonds and candied orange peel (see recipe on page 31).

Blanch the almonds by plunging them in boiling water for a few minutes. Their brown skins will then rub off very easily. Crush the nuts with the candied orange peel in a pestle and mortar or in a food processor, whichever you prefer. You should obtain a grainy paste. Add 2 tablespoons of honey to bind the paste. When it is evenly mixed, pour it on to a sheet of rice paper that you have laid on a baking sheet. Spread the paste to form a layer 1 cm (½ inch) thick. In a bowl, beat 3 egg whites with 300 g (10 oz) of icing sugar until you get a smooth and fluid royal icing. Spread it over the almond and orange paste. Cut the *calissons* into diamond-shaped pieces and bake them in a very low oven for 5 minutes.

The Thirteen 'Desserts'
~

WINE:
Muscat de
Beaumes-
de-Venise

Throughout Provence, each family has its own traditional selection of 'desserts', but you need 13 'desserts' without fail, in memory of Christ and his 12 apostles. I should explain that originally 'desserts' meant nuts and dried fruits served at the end of a meal. Everyone agrees on the 4 *mendiants* (beggars): golden sultanas to represent the Dominican monks, almonds to symbolize the bare-footed Carmelites, hazelnuts for the Augustine robes, and dried figs for the Franciscans. Most people include dates and nuts, and black and white nougat. On the other hand, the choice of fruit varies from one family to another: oranges are sometimes replaced with mandarins, sometimes it is pears or apples, green grapes miraculously preserved in the attic or a melon suspended since September in a net to keep it safe from man and beast. In Marseilles, they make olive oil bread, in Aix there is *gibassié*, and in Orange the butter *fougasse*. In Vaison-la-Romaine they make apple panade – this is a kind of tart made of bread dough enriched with butter, topped with grated apple and decorated with a lattice made of dough. The panade is flavoured with a few drops of orange-flower water when it comes out of the oven, crusty and golden. To all this, you can add quince paste (see page 27), candied orange and lemon peel (see page 31), *calissons* (see page 69) and sometimes even grapes marinated in fruit brandy (see below). With these 13 'desserts', we serve *carthagène* (see recipe on page 121) or a muscat wine from Beaumes-de-Venise.

Grapes in Eau-de-vie
~

To make this alcohol preserve, choose firm white grapes. With a pair of scissors, separate each grape from the bunch, leaving a 5 mm (¼ inch) stalk on each one. Wipe the grapes carefully and put them in a sterilized jar. Then fill the jar with a good fruit brandy. Add 2 tablespoons of sugar per litre (1¾ pints). Seal the jar, lock it away in a dark cupboard or secret place and forget about it for a year.

FROM CHRISTMAS
TO NEW YEAR

The Christmas supper is over and it is time to go to midnight mass. You will eat the leftover *fougasse* tomorrow morning for breakfast, with a large cup of warming milky coffee. But do not eat too much, because Christmas Day lunch should be full of surprises. It must be a real feast and, for once, we are going to forget the usual simplicity of Provençal cooking. We will buy a plump, white-fleshed chicken from Bresse and a duck foie gras from neighbouring Languedoc. At the Carpentras market, we will buy our truffles. Everything else, we have on hand.

Artichoke Salad
~

Choose 12 plump and firm artichoke bottoms. As you clean each one, rub it with lemon juice and then immediately drop it into a bowl of water, to prevent it from turning black. In a pan mix 1 tablespoon of flour with 2 tablespoons of vinegar (or lemon juice) and then stir in 1 litre (1¾ pints) of cold, lightly salted water. Bring the water to the boil, stirring constantly. Add the artichoke bottoms and simmer until just cooked, but still a little crunchy. Drain and then pat the artichokes dry.

In a bowl, prepare a vinaigrette with extra-virgin olive oil, a touch of good quality wine vinegar and some sea salt. Brush and peel 2 or 3 truffles. Reserve the peel to use in the chicken stuffing. Cut the truffles into thick slices.

On each plate, make a bed of lamb's lettuce, and arrange 2 artichoke bottoms on top. Place a slice of pink foie gras and a slice of truffle on each portion. Pour 1 tablespoon of vinaigrette over each artichoke. It is simple but so delicious!

WINE:
Crozes
Hermitage
rouge

Poached Chicken

~

WINE:
Crozes
Hermitage
rouge

The day before you are going to cook the chicken you need to prepare and stuff it. First, clean the chicken thoroughly. Then prepare the stuffing. Mince 500 g (1 lb) of veal with the liver of the chicken, 100 g (3½ oz) of foie gras and 1–2 truffles. Mix all this with 1 tablespoon of olive oil and 3 tablespoons of cognac. Season with sea salt and freshly ground pepper. Stuff and truss the chicken. Keep it in the refrigerator until ready to cook.

Place the chicken in a cooking pot just large enough to hold it. Add 2 carrots, 1 onion studded with cloves, a small bunch of parsley, some sprigs of thyme, a bay leaf and a leek. Cover with cold water or chicken stock and season with a pinch of salt. Poach the chicken, covered, over a very low heat for 1½–2 hours.

Fifteen minutes before serving, melt 20 g (³⁄₄ oz) of butter in a saucepan. Add 1 tablespoon of flour, stir and cook for a few minutes, but do not let the flour brown. Take the pan off the heat and little by little add about 300 ml (½ pint) of the stock in which you have poached the chicken, stirring constantly. Beat well with a whisk, and return to the heat. Bring to the boil and keep stirring until thickened. Cook for a few minutes longer. Then add 6 tablespoons of fresh double cream. Off the heat, mix 2 egg yolks, 1 tablespoon of lemon juice and a little grated nutmeg in a bowl. Slowly pour the sauce into the egg mixture, stirring constantly. Return to the pan and heat the sauce – but do not allow it to boil. Finish off the sauce by stirring in a knob of fresh butter.

Serve the chicken with Creole rice (boiled rice) and the sauce served separately in a warmed sauce-boat.

New Year's Day
Lentils

~

For the 1st of January, the only recipe I will give you is for a dish of lentils so that you will be rich all year. In our family (I do not know where the tradition comes from), we say that 'if you eat lentils on the 1st of January, you will have money all year'. I think it is a wise, even delicious, tradition and so I have always observed it.

*Poache
Chicke*

IN THE KITCHEN : In a large pan cook 200 g (7 oz) of chopped onions in a little olive oil until they are soft. Add 500 g (1 lb) of thickly sliced leeks, 500 g (1 lb) of diced potatoes, 400 g (13 oz) of country sausages, pricked with a fork so they will not burst while cooking, and 500 g (1 lb) of green or brown lentils, picked over and washed. Cover with cold water – about 3 litres (5 pints). Add a dozen unpeeled garlic cloves, some sea salt and freshly ground black pepper. Cover, bring to the boil, then lower the heat and simmer for at least an hour. Just before serving, add a knob of fresh butter. Drain the lentils and the vegetables.

Serve the broth first in warm soup bowls with garlic toast and grated cheese. Then serve the lentils, the vegetables and the sausages.

'Baïano'
of Chickpeas
~

Here is a meal very similar to the dish of New Year's Day lentils. It's a chickpea soup, eaten traditionally on Palm Sunday when the winter chickpea reserves were getting low. But before telling you about this recipe, let me tell you the best way to cook chickpeas. If you cook them in water that has been used for cooking spinach, you do not need to soak them overnight or add bicarbonate of soda to the water to soften them.

IN THE KITCHEN : If you have not eaten spinach the day before, soak about 450 g (14–15 oz) of chickpeas in water overnight with a pinch of bicarbonate of soda. Drain them and rinse them several times. Then place them in a cooking pot with 3 litres (5 pints) of water, 2 leeks, 1 carrot, 1 handful of spinach leaves (to facilitate the cooking), 2 garlic cloves, 1 bay leaf, 2 sage leaves, some sea salt and freshly ground pepper. When the liquid starts boiling, skim it carefully, then lower the heat, cover the pot and simmer for at least 2 hours, until the peas are really tender. Add 500 g (1 lb) of little country sausages (pricked with a fork) for the last 30 minutes. When the chickpeas are cooked, take out the sausages and slice them. Drain the chickpeas and keep the broth. Serve it in warm soup bowls with garlic toast and slices of sausage. Sprinkle with grated cheese. Then serve the chickpeas with an *aïoli* (see recipe on page 184) or simply with a good olive oil vinaigrette.

My Mother's
Almond Log

~

Please do not be discouraged by the word 'log' and definitely try this truly delicious cake, flavoured with coffee and almonds. It must be prepared the day before it is served.

First, make a pot of very good, very strong coffee and then let it cool.

Allow 250 g (8 oz) of butter to soften in a warm place.

Take about 30 whole almonds, soak them for several minutes in boiling water, then drain. Dry the nuts and rub off their skins. Roast the nuts in a hot oven for about 5 minutes, until they are golden. Do not allow the nuts to burn or they will taste bitter. Once cool place the almonds in a strong paper bag and crush them with a rolling pin. Set them aside.

In a large bowl, beat the softened butter with 5 tablespoons of icing sugar. When the mixture is pale and smooth, beat in 1 egg yolk and then gradually add some of the cold coffee, until you have flavoured the cream to your taste.

Take some sponge fingers and dip them quickly in the remaining coffee (be careful not to soak them too much). Make the cake by alternating layers of sponge fingers and buttercream, and forming it into the shape of a log. Remember you will need to reserve about half the buttercream for the outside of the log. When you have covered the log with buttercream, decorate the top with the crushed almonds so it resembles the bark of a tree (but not the ends, which are supposed to be the wood of the tree).

Store the cake in a cool place, but not in the refrigerator, until the following day.

U NDER A
W INTER'S S UN

There are winter days, blessed days when suddenly the mistral vanishes, after having blown across the country night and day, taking advantage of every lane, every doorway, every crack in the wood to spread its freezing breath. But all of a sudden, everything stops moving. The sun bursts out through the clouds, flooding the landscape. On these days you must make the best of this gift from heaven.

The stone walls of the Bidaine *pavillon*, still showing the remains of their centuries-old ochre colour, suddenly take on the most beautiful shade under the light of this pale winter sun. But the light is even more magical inside the yellow sitting room, opening to the south on to a garden of ornamental ponds, to the east on to the orchards and the flower garden, and to the north on to a trimmed boxwood walk. Seven high french windows, framed with sulphur yellow Chinese pelmets look out on to the gardens. A long couch, a few wing chairs, small occasional tables and a harpsichord are the only furniture in this living room, which invites you to relax and enjoy life under the impassive gaze of two painted clay mandarins which seem to have been there for eternity.

What about lunch in this yellow sitting room? Not at a set table but rather a picnic. We will open wide the seven windows of the room, as if it were summer. We will make *oreillettes* (sweet fritters), dried fruit compote, gingerbread cream, and we will drink muscat from Beaumes-de-Venise. We could eat an egg soup or stuffed eggs, and carrot and beef stew. What a wonderful idea! We could even dress up in 18th-century attire, in richly embroidered silk waistcoats, and Ted could play the harpsichord.

And this is how, one February day, we came to have a picnic in the yellow sitting room, dressed up in 18th-century clothes, enjoying the warmth of the winter sun.

Beef Olives

Egg Soup
~

In the old days, every meal started with a soup, and often it was the only plentiful dish of the meal. The one feature common to all these soups was the large slice of bread, sometimes rubbed with a garlic clove, always sprinkled with *le râpé* (grated cheese) that would melt in the hot broth. You find it in fish soup, as well as in lentil soup, in salt cod *bouill-abaisse* and in egg soup.

IN THE KITCHEN : The recipe for egg soup begins like the *aïgo boulido* from the Christmas Eve supper. In a pot of salted water add as many as 3 or 4 garlic cloves per person, left unpeeled and crushed slightly. Let the water boil for about 10 minutes. Turn off the heat, add a bay leaf, a sprig of thyme, a few sage leaves, cover with a lid and let the flavours infuse until the liquid is cold.

Now you must strain the broth into a clean pan and warm it up again without letting it boil. Then you make a little *aïoli* (see recipe on page 184) and mix it into the broth.

Serve with grated cheese and the toasted bread, of course. That is the traditional recipe, but at home, we also make egg soup with any kind of broth: vegetable, chicken or beef. Try it – it is delicious.

'Brouillade' with Truffles
~

WINE :
Hermitage
blanc

The day before, grate the truffle (or truffles) finely, place it in a bowl and cover it with a small glass of virgin olive oil. When you want to cook the *brouillade* (scrambled eggs), beat the eggs, add the truffle and oil, some sea salt and freshly ground pepper and pour into a pan on a double-boiler. Cook for about 20 minutes, stirring constantly. When the eggs reach the consistency of thick cream, take the pan off the heat – it is crucial that the eggs remain moist and creamy. Add a good tablespoon of cream and keep stirring. Transfer the *brouillade* to a serving dish straight away or it will go on cooking. This cooking method is a little tricky but it is well worth it. Serve the *brouillade* nice and hot with a little lamb's lettuce salad.

Stuffed Eggs

~

Allow 2 eggs per person. Hard boil them, peel them and cut them in half. Remove the yolks and place the white part, cut side up, in a baking dish. In a pan, over a low heat, cook 2 onions, finely sliced, in a mixture of butter and olive oil until they are soft – do not let them colour too much. While the onions are cooking, wash and trim 500 g (1 lb) of spinach leaves. Blanch the leaves in boiling salted water for 3 minutes. Drain, squeezing out as much liquid as you can. Then chop the spinach fairly finely and mix with the onion, the hard-boiled egg yolks, a little milk, and some sea salt and freshly ground pepper. Fill the egg whites with this stuffing, sprinkle grated cheese on top, then pour a light white sauce over the eggs. Brown in a hot oven for 15 minutes.

Spinach and Sardine Tian

~

Trim and wash some young spinach leaves. Blanch for 5 minutes in boiling salted water, then drain, squeeze out as much liquid as you can and chop the leaves roughly. In a pan brown a chopped onion in a little olive oil. Add the chopped spinach and 2 chopped garlic cloves. Sprinkle over 1 tablespoon of flour. Add a little hot milk, sea salt and freshly ground pepper and mix with a spoon. Pour the spinach mixture into a baking dish.

Take 20 good-sized sardines, cut off their heads, clean them and fillet them. Place the fish on top of the spinach, sprinkle over some grated cheese and breadcrumbs. Drizzle with a little olive oil and brown in a hot oven for 15 minutes.

WINE: Côtes de Provence blanc

Potato and
Spinach Tian

~

I do not know where this recipe came from, possibly from Nice, from Alsace, or maybe it was my mother's own creation. Anyway, it was one of my favourite dishes when I was a child, and I give it to you the way my mother gave it to me. Peel 1 kg (2 lb) of potatoes and slice them thickly. Place them in a pan of cold water and bring them to the boil. Then turn off the heat. Remove the potatoes with a slotted spoon and spread them in a gratin dish. Sprinkle a handful of chopped bacon and 2 onions, finely sliced, over the potatoes. Cover them with 500 g (1 lb) of blanched spinach leaves (do not forget to squeeze out as much water as possible). Pour boiling milk seasoned with salt and freshly ground pepper over the gratin to cover the spinach. Bake in a moderate oven for about 45 minutes.

Daube from Avignon

~

The traditional pot used to cook this stew is a *daubière*, a large, round, glazed earthenware dish with a lid. The oldest ones appear scorched by days of simmering in the hearth. My clay pot, which I still have today, is shallow enough to fit in my oven. The lid of the *daubière* must have a little hole in it to let the steam escape during cooking. I make a kind of thick ribbon of dough with flour and water to seal the lid to the pot. The cooking is done in a slow oven and all the flavours are trapped in the *daubière*.

WINE: Châteauneuf-du-Pape blanc

This cooking method is perfect for all dishes that need to be simmered. But of course, they can be made just as successfully on a gas stove if you use a heavy-bottomed pot with a metal plate underneath to diffuse the heat.

IN THE KITCHEN : Bone a leg of lamb and cut the meat into large cubes (the size of an egg). Alternatively you could ask the butcher to do this for you. Place the meat in the pot. Add the bone as well, with 1 piece of thick streaky bacon, diced. The following ingredients also need to be added to the *daubière*: 2 chopped onions, 2 sliced carrots, a dozen unpeeled garlic cloves, a bay leaf, 3 pieces of dried orange peel, a generous pinch of grated nutmeg and 1 bottle of white Châteauneuf-du-Pape. Season with salt and freshly ground pepper.

Let the lamb marinate for 6 hours, then simmer in a slow oven for 2½ hours. Remove the bone and serve straight from the *daubière*.

Braised Beef
with Carrots

~

Have your butcher prepare a nice roast of stewing beef, weighing approximately 1.5 kg (3 lb), wrapped in bacon. Dice 1 piece of streaky bacon and brown in a heavy-bottomed pot with a little olive oil and a little butter. When the fat is really hot, quickly but carefully seal and brown the meat over a high heat. Pour 1 cup of dry white wine over it and let it reduce for a few minutes. Lower the heat and cover the pot.

After 1 hour, add 1 kg (2 lb) of carrots, thickly sliced, 2 onions, sliced, a stick of celery and a large garlic clove, both chopped finely. If in season, you can add a chopped tomato, but never use tomato sauce or tinned tomatoes.

Cooking takes about 3 hours. Towards the end, you can add black olives or cooked morel mushrooms, but only at the last minute.

WINE: Lirac rouge

Pages 82–83:
The large yellow
living room of
the Bidaine
pavillon

'Brouffade' from the River Rhône

~

Here is an old recipe for beef with anchovies and capers, well known on the banks of the Rhône, from Arles to Lyon. You will need a large earthenware cooking pot which will fit in your oven and a large *tian* in which to marinate the meat. The night before, slice 1.5 kg (3 lb) of stewing beef into fairly thin slices. Marinate the beef overnight in 4 tablespoons of olive oil, 2 bay leaves, 6 cloves of garlic, lightly crushed, 2 cloves and a pinch of freshly grated nutmeg.

WINE: Laudun blanc

The following day, take the meat out of the marinade. Strain the marinade, reserving the oil and the garlic. Finely slice 2–3 large onions and mix them with the garlic from the marinade. Add 100 g (3½ oz) of drained capers and 12 pickled gherkins, chopped.

Using a pestle and mortar, mash 6 anchovy fillets with 1 tablespoon of flour. Thin the paste with 2 tablespoons of wine vinegar and the oil from the marinade. Transfer the anchovy paste to a large bowl, add the meat and stir to coat. Season lightly with sea salt and generously with freshly ground black pepper.

In the earthenware cooking pot, alternate layers of the onion and caper mixture, with layers of meat in anchovy sauce until the dish is full. Pour 2 cups of water over the meat. Seal the lid of the pot with a ribbon of dough made with flour and water. Bake in a medium-hot oven until the *brouffade* is boiling, then reduce the oven temperature to maintain a slow simmer. The *brouffade* should cook for at least 3 hours.

Beef Olives

~

Ask your butcher to cut thin slices of topside, about 5 x 7 cm (2 x 3 inches), allowing 3 slices for each person. On each slice, place a small piece of bacon and ½ teaspoon of chopped garlic and parsley. Roll the beef slices around the bacon and tie them up with a piece of string. The beef olives are ready. This is a simple but delicious dish.

In a heavy-bottomed pan, pour a little olive oil and add 1 carrot and 1 onion, finely sliced. Place the beef olives on top. Brown over a medium heat. When the vegetables start catching a bit, add a glass of dry white wine, and let the wine reduce for a few minutes, before adding 2 glasses of stock, a bay leaf, a sprig of thyme, a piece of dried orange peel, 2 unpeeled garlic cloves and the chopped-up flesh of 2 ripe tomatoes (but no tomato sauce). Cover the pan and cook over a low heat for 2 hours.

WINE: Lirac rouge

My Godmother Lilou's Fennel Compote

~

Julienne (cut into fine strips) a few fennel bulbs and an equal number of onions. In a heavy-bottomed pan, brown the onions lightly in a little olive oil. Then add the fennel, a drop of water, a pinch of salt, some freshly ground pepper and 2 teaspoons of mild paprika. Stir well, cover and simmer for about 20 minutes, until very soft.

Serve the fennel piping hot, with a celeriac purée (see recipe on page 87), to accompany roast beef.

White Chicory Compote
~

It is not necessary to wash the chicory but do wipe them carefully. Slice them thinly and discard the inner core at the root end.

In a large frying pan, over a low heat, cook the chicory in butter until all the water has evaporated and they are starting to dry out. Add some sea salt and freshly ground pepper and 1 tablespoon of caster sugar and let them brown. Cover and cook over a low heat for about 20 minutes, until the chicory has softened completely.

Just before serving, add the juice of half a lemon and 2 tablespoons of fresh single cream.

This compote is a perfect accompaniment to roast veal or grilled fish.

Mashed Potatoes with Leeks
~

Carefully wash 500 g (1 lb) of the white part of leeks and cut them into 1 cm (½ inch) thick slices. Cook the leeks in salted water for about 20 minutes, then drain.

Wash and peel 1 kg (2 lb) of potatoes and cook them in salted water until they are tender. Drain and mash. Add hot milk, little by little, until the mashed potatoes are smooth but not too runny. You are not making a soup!

Add the drained leeks, a tablespoon of butter, some freshly ground pepper and a pinch of grated nutmeg. Taste and add a little sea salt if necessary.

Serve with roast fowl.

Celeriac Purée

~

Wash and peel 700 g (1 lb 7 oz) of potatoes and 700 g (1 lb 7 oz) of celeriac (1 or 2 roots) and cut both vegetables into large pieces.

Boil the celeriac and potatoes together in salted water until they are soft, then drain and mash them. Add just enough hot milk and cream to make a smooth, light purée. Season with freshly ground pepper, and sea salt if necessary.

Serve with red meat or game.

Rosette's Rice Pudding

~

This is a very easy pudding to make. All you need is 1 litre (1¾ pints) of fresh whole milk, 5 tablespoons of Camargue round rice (short-grain rice), 16 sugar cubes, 1 vanilla pod and 1 teaspoon of butter. Put all these ingredients together in a saucepan, place over a low heat and slowly bring to the boil, stirring frequently. Remove from the heat and pour the mixture into an ovenproof baking dish. Bake the rice pudding for at least 2 hours in a cool oven.

The secret of this dish is slow cooking. The top of the pudding should brown slightly but the underneath should remain creamy, almost like the delicious 'milk jam' they make in Argentina.

Edith's Orange and Caramel Salad

~

My friend Edith is a wonderful embroiderer, but she is also an exceptional cook. When she makes an orange salad, she cannot resist embroidering the top with threads of caramel. It is both gorgeous and delicious!

I<small>N THE KITCHEN</small> : Peel 7 large oranges, carefully removing all the pith as

well as the skin. Slice the flesh thinly into rounds. Arrange the orange slices in a shallow serving dish.

Make a caramel with 25 sugar cubes and a drop of water (see recipe on page 41). When the caramel is golden, remove from the heat; do not let it burn or it will taste bitter. Cool the caramel by adding a drop of cold water. Wait a few seconds for it to thicken slightly, moving the saucepan constantly. Do not wait too long or the caramel will harden completely. So, as soon as it has thickened, pour this caramel over the oranges from fairly high up – the way they serve tea in Morocco. That way, the toffee will have time to cool on the way down so it will be easier to make a nice design on the oranges.

Serve the salad fairly soon after making it, because if you wait too long, the juice of the fruit will dissolve the caramel.

Madame Pavan's
'Oreillettes'

~

Theresa Pavan is Italian. She used to be the cook, and is still a friend, of the Duchess of Sabran-Pontèves in Château d'Ansouis. During one of many marvellous meals, Theresa made *oreillettes* (fritters) – like nobody else. She knew I loved them, and ever since Theresa has sent me a basketful of *oreillettes* on Pancake Tuesday, every year. Here is her recipe.

IN THE KITCHEN : Make a dough by mixing together 500 g (1 lb) of flour, 150 g (5 oz) of caster sugar, a pinch of salt, 1 tablespoon of orange-flower water, a knob of soft butter, 4 egg yolks and 150 ml (¼ pint) of milk. Do not work the dough too much. Form it into a ball and let it rest in a cool place for 2 hours.

If you own a pasta-making machine, roll out the dough as for lasagne. If not, use a rolling pin to roll out the dough until it is 2 mm (¹⁄₁₀ inch) thick. Cut out strips of dough measuring 15 cm (6 inches) by 7 cm (3 inches) and make an incision in the middle of each strip. Deep-fry the *oreillettes* in peanut oil, take them out as soon as they are golden and let them drain on kitchen paper. Sprinkle them with icing sugar or caster sugar. In the old days, they would have been fried in olive oil in a frying pan. I tried it and it is delicious but the flavour was a little strong.

Véronique L.'s
Dried Fruit Compote
~

WINE:
Côtes
du Rhône
Rasteau
moelleux

Heavenly Véronique, who looks as though she has just stepped out of a Watteau painting, is swirling in her dress, laughing, and leaning over to one side while she dips a dried apricot into gingerbread cream.

IN THE KITCHEN : Place 300 g (10 oz) of stoned prunes, 300 g (10 oz) of stoned dates and 300 g (10 oz) of dried apricots in a saucepan. Cover them with 200 ml (7 fl oz) of tea, the juice and the grated rind of 2 oranges, a generous pinch of powdered cinnamon and 4 tablespoons of honey. Cover and cook over a low heat for 15 minutes. Take the pan off the heat and add 300 g (10 oz) of pine nuts. Pour into a pretty compote dish and leave for a few hours before serving with honey ice cream or gingerbread cream.

Véronique L.'s
Gingerbread Cream
~

Wash 50 g (2 oz) of sultanas and let them soak in boiling water for 10 minutes. In a saucepan, bring to the boil 250 ml (8 fl oz) of milk, 400 ml (14 fl oz) of single cream and a vanilla pod, split in two. Remove from the heat and leave to infuse for 10 minutes.

In a large bowl, mix 1 tablespoon of honey with 2 egg yolks and 1 teaspoon of green aniseed. Gradually stir the hot milk and cream into the egg and honey mixture. Strain and then return the liquid to a clean pan and cook over a very low heat until the cream thickens, stirring all the time.

In a deep dish, crumble 400 g (13 oz) of very good gingerbread, pour the boiling hot cream over it and beat with a balloon whisk until the mixture is smooth. Add the drained plump sultanas. Allow the cream to cool, then chill in the refrigerator for about 3 hours before serving.

Dried Fr
Compote a
Gingerbre
Cre

A Spring Lunch

For a long time lamb has been an indispensable part of our Easter lunch. When people had huge fireplaces, they used to roast a whole lamb – the *Pascal* lamb. Now, most of us make do with just a leg. But the fact remains that the best way to cook this roast is on a spit over a log fire. You need some nice oak logs, and in front of the fire an antique spit, which will turn the meat slowly before the flames. They are extremely simple but most of them still work beautifully. So skewer your leg of lamb on the spit, without studding it with garlic cloves or anchovies, because the slits would allow the meat juices to escape. For the same reason, salt it only towards the end of cooking. Just before salting it, 'flame' it. I will tell you how to 'flame' it by sharing another nice story: the tale of the *brochette* of thrush.

It happened one winter, in a beautiful fireplace in Vinsobres, at the boundary between the Drôme and the Vaucluse. The men had killed the birds and the women had prepared them by cutting off their feet, plucking out all the feathers, and then holding them over a flame for a few seconds to burn off the down. The men had kindled the fire, then they had skewered the birds, belly up, heads pointing towards the outside of the spit, because as Jeannot explained, 'when they turn, they drip and when they drip, the juices run down the beak and drip on to the bread'. The 'bread' consisted of large slices of bread, placed immediately under the roast on a dripping pan.

WINE:
Vinsobres
rouge or
Côte Rôtie

So, they had placed the birds on the spit, heads up, and interspersed here and there with a few nice pieces of pork belly because, Jeannot went on, 'there are always those who are not keen on thrush so there is no waste'. The birds were seasoned with a little salt and freshly ground pepper, and then all that remained was to cook them in front of a steady fire for about 3 hours – not forgetting to move the slices of bread around from time to time. They were all looking at the spit turning slowly, waiting for the moment to flame the birds. To do this, they used a kind of metal funnel on which a handle had been soldered. The funnel was placed in the fire to heat it up. When it was red hot, and the birds were almost cooked, a piece of bacon fat was placed inside the funnel. The bacon melted instantly into a kind of rain of fat that showered all over the birds. The birds were then served on the bread and, believe me, soon only 'the beak and the tail' were left.

But this is spring, the table is set in the garden, and besides the leg of lamb, I have prepared a nice green salad, some asparagus from Lauris with a 'simple' little sauce, a dish of morels and sausages, all the lovely spring vegetables from the garden, a superb strawberry cake and some unusual acacia fritters.

Lauris Asparagus
with Truffles

~

As for the *brouillade*, or scrambled eggs (see recipe on page 78), you will have to grate the truffles finely the day before and let them marinate overnight in a glass of olive oil.

The following day, just before serving, you need to add a little salt and freshly ground pepper, and a dash of wine vinegar. Now you have the perfect sauce to go with your beautiful asparagus from Lauris.

Choose thick white asparagus with green and purple tips. Carefully wash and peel the base of the asparagus (do not touch the fragile tips). Cook the asparagus in boiling salted water for about 15 minutes – they will need a little longer if they are really big. But be careful, because asparagus

should not be overcooked; they should remain just firm to the bite. Serve them warm with the truffle vinaigrette.

Wild Asparagus
Omelette

~

In Provence you can find wild asparagus in the spring, growing under bushes and in the vineyards. They grow into long, slender, curved stems, and you should use only about 20 cm (8 inches) from the tip.

Blanch the asparagus for 10 minutes in boiling salted water, and then drain. With a fork, scrape away the hard parts at the bottom of the stems and cut the remaining asparagus into 10 cm (4 inch) strips. Pour a little olive oil into a frying pan, and brown the asparagus strips over a medium heat for 5 minutes. Add some beaten eggs, salt and freshly ground pepper, and sprinkle with some grated Dutch cheese – *le rouge*.

Allow the eggs to cook for a few minutes on one side, stirring occasionally with a wooden spoon, then flip the omelette over and cook it on the other side.

To flip the eggs over, you can use a traditional Provençal *vire-omelette* ('omelette flipper') which is an invaluable disc of glazed clay (see illustration on page 140). If you do not have one, just use a pan lid.

Green Salad
~

It was traditional in Provence to start lunch with a green salad, which was always served with a vinaigrette, made with olive oil, according to the '4 people' rule: a miser for the vinegar, a wise man for the salt and pepper, a rich man for the oil and a mad man to mix it.

IN THE KITCHEN : With lamb's lettuce, called *doucette* in Provence, add to the basic '4 people' vinaigrette, 2 finely sliced onions which have been cooked slowly until soft and translucent in olive oil.

With curly endive, use the same vinaigrette and serve with garlic croûtons which should be added just before mixing the salad, or they will be soggy. You can also add a few matchsticks of celery.

With dandelion leaves or wild herbs that you have picked in the country or bought at the market, flavour the vinaigrette with 2–3 anchovy fillets and 1 garlic clove, both finely crushed.

With Cos or round lettuce, add a few finely chopped spring onions or olives, and decorate with slices of hard-boiled egg.

Finally, with rocket, add some shavings of very dry Banon goats' cheese to the vinaigrette, and use lemon juice instead of vinegar. Shavings of Parmesan cheese are delicious too.

Cos lettuce and
lettuce hearts

Pages 98–99
Jacques Grange
Mas Mireio

Salad of Purple
Artichokes from Villelaure
~

This is another spring salad which is slightly bitter, but very delicate in flavour. Clean some baby purple artichokes from Villelaure, and slice them finely. Pour some lemon juice over them straight away, mix well and add some olive oil, salt and freshly ground pepper. That is all, and it is really, really good!

Artichoke
Omelette
~

Select some small purple artichokes, tear off and discard the hard outer leaves and the stem. Cut the artichokes in half. Remove the chokes if there are any, but if the artichokes are young, there should not be very much. Slice them finely and cook in olive oil until golden. When they are ready, use as the basis for an omelette, following the recipe on page 95, for Wild Asparagus Omelette.

Homemade
Ravioli
~

This ravioli is large and square, made of dough which is filled and then cooked in boiling water. It has nothing to do with the tiny ravioli from the town of Romans, which is a delicious version, generally served as a first course and which I personally prefer pan-fried until nice and crunchy, and served with drinks (see recipe on page 127).

IN THE KITCHEN : Start by making the dough: place 500 g (1 lb) of plain flour on a smooth work surface and make a well in the centre. Break 5 eggs into the well (as a general rule, you need 1 egg for every 100 g (3½ oz) of flour). Add a generous pinch of salt and 3 tablespoons of olive oil, then mix with your fingers to form a dough. Lightly knead the dough until it is smooth and elastic; this will take 5–10 minutes. Allow the dough to rest for an hour.

Meanwhile, we will prepare the filling. I am going to give you 3 delicious recipes, all of them using fresh young spinach leaves which have been blanched for a few minutes in boiling salted water, drained, squeezed, and then chopped finely.

First, a classic recipe – Meat Ravioli. For this, use 300 g (10 oz) of leftover *daube* or stewed beef. Mince the meat and then mix it with an equal quantity of finely chopped, blanched spinach. Finely chop 2 onions and cook them in a little olive oil over a low heat until golden. Add the onions with 3 egg yolks to the meat and spinach filling. Mix together and season to taste.

Another classic recipe – Cheese Ravioli. Mix together 300 g (10 oz) of fresh *brousse* cheese with 100 g (3½ oz) of grated Gruyère cheese and 3 egg yolks. Add 300 g (10 oz) of finely chopped, blanched spinach. Season to taste.

Finally, a more original recipe which personally I like very much – Ravioli with Mussels. Cook 1 cob of sweetcorn in boiling salted water until tender, then remove the kernels. Place the kernels in a food processor or blender and liquidize. Clean 1 litre (1¾ pints) of live mussels, by scrubbing their shells and removing their 'beards'. Put them in a covered pot over a high heat with a chopped garlic clove and a dash of olive oil. Cook the mussels for a few minutes until the shells open, discarding any mussels that remain closed. Let the mussels cool, then carefully remove them from their shells and mix them with 300 g (10 oz) of finely chopped, blanched spinach, the creamed sweetcorn and 3 egg yolks. Season to taste.

Now, for the dough, ideally you would use a pasta-making machine, but you can also use a rolling pin. Roll out the dough on a floured surface to form sheets, about 1 mm (⅛ inch) thick.

Cut each sheet into a 7 cm (3 inch) square. On half of these squares, place 1 tablespoon of the filling you have chosen, then cover with another square of dough. Seal the ravioli all around with your fingers.

Bring a large saucepan of water to the boil, add a handful of salt and 1 tablespoon of oil. Cook the ravioli in the boiling water. They are ready when they float to the surface. As they are ready, carefully take them out with a slotted spoon and serve them straight away, simply with a dash of olive oil drizzled over them. A stronger sauce would mask their delicate flavour.

Leg of Lamb with
Garlic Cream Sauce

~

WINE:
Côtes
du Luberon
rouge

Ideally roast your leg of lamb on a spit over an open oak fire. Alternatively coat it lightly with oil and bake it in a hot oven. Allow 20 minutes for each 500 g (1 lb) of meat.

Meanwhile, boil about 10 whole heads of garlic, still in their skins. After 10 minutes, throw the water away and replace it with fresh boiling water. Cook the garlic for a further 10 minutes. Remove the garlic and allow it to cool. Then peel the bulbs, discarding the skin and mashing the flesh.

When the lamb is cooked, place on a warmed serving plate, and sprinkle with sea salt. Then deglaze the meat juices with a little hot water, scraping in all the brown meat extracts. Add the mashed garlic and stir until well mixed. Serve this creamy garlic sauce in a warmed sauce-boat with the carved lamb.

Roast Kid
with Anchovies

~

WINE:
Côtes
du Luberon
rouge

You will find that good quality kid meat is available around Easter. Kid meat is best roasted but requires stronger seasoning than lamb.

As when cooking lamb, roast it on a spit or in the oven. Place a few lemon slices around the meat, with 10–12 garlic cloves, still in their skins, 10–12 anchovy fillets, 1 glass of water and a few cubes of streaky bacon. If you are roasting the meat, do it in a hot oven, allowing about 20 minutes per 500 g (1 lb). Baste and turn it several times, and salt towards the end of cooking. Add a little water from time to time, if necessary.

When the roast is ready transfer it to a warm serving platter. Discard the lemon slices. Remove the garlic cloves, peel them and return to the roasting tin. Deglaze the roasting tin with a little boiling water, mashing the garlic and the anchovies into the gravy. Serve with the roast.

A Stew of
Spring Vegetables
~

Have you ever been at the market of l'Isle-sur-la-Sorgue, a large wicker basket on your arm, on a beautiful spring morning? I know I am overly partial to this market, as well as those in Carpentras and Saint-Rémy, and I apologize. In fact, all the Provence markets are wonderful. In the spring, the River Sorgue is high and clear, the sun shines brightly through the young leaves on the trees, and the air is cool and light. The market stalls are piled high displaying gorgeous greens and new spring vegetables. They are so appetizing, so tender, so pink, so green that you do not know which to choose. The broad beans or the carrots, the tiny purple artichokes (picked from the plant so that more can grow), the translucent mangetout or the baby onions, white and plump. The first thought that springs into my mind is, let's make a delicious stew of new spring vegetables.

IN THE KITCHEN : You will need a selection of all these lovely young vegetables: potatoes, carrots, little white onions, peas, broad beans, mangetout, small purple artichokes and lettuce hearts.

Wash them carefully. Do not peel the potatoes or the artichokes and only scrape the carrots if absolutely necessary. Remove the outer skin of the onions, shell the peas and the broad beans and clean the lettuce hearts. Place all the vegetables in a heavy-bottomed pan with 3 tablespoons of fruity olive oil, 3 tablespoons of water, a pinch of caster sugar, some sea salt and freshly ground pepper. Cover the pan and let the vegetables cook slowly for 30 minutes.

Morels with Pork Sausages

~

WINE:
Séguret
rouge

In the spring, in the sandy soil of the Luberon foothills, you can pick basketfuls of *mourigoulo*, morel mushrooms. In l'Isle-sur-la-Sorgue, we eat them with long, thin fresh pork sausages which we call *saucissettes*, and which are absolutely delicious grilled.

IN THE KITCHEN : Cut off the sandy part at the base of the morels. Wash them carefully and dry them well. Cut the larger mushrooms into 2–3 pieces.
You will need 2 sausages for each person. Prick them with a fork, so that they will not burst when cooking. Brown the sausages in a frying pan to render some of their fat.

When the sausages are cooked, remove from the pan and keep them warm.
Add a small piece of butter and 1 tablespoon of olive oil to the pan. When the fat is hot, add the mushrooms. Season with sea salt and freshly ground pepper. Allow the mushrooms to cook until all the water has evaporated. Return the sausages to the pan with the morels and warm them through for 2 minutes. Sprinkle with chopped parsley and serve piping hot.
You can make the same dish in the autumn, using different mushrooms, such as milk mushrooms, which benefit from the addition of a little chopped garlic with the parsley.

Artichokes 'en Barigoule'

~

The Provençal word for mushroom is *barigoulo* or *berigoulo*. This is also the word for the wide-brimmed felt hats which country women used to wear. It also describes a way of cooking artichokes, probably because the artichokes in this recipe end up looking a little like mushrooms.

IN THE KITCHEN : Use 2 kg (4 lb) of small, tender, purple artichokes. Discard the tough outer leaves. Using a sharp knife, cut off the top of the artichokes, then cut them into halves or quarters, depending on their size. Remove and discard any chokes, but if the artichokes are

*Morels with
Pork Sausa[ges]*

really small, they will not have one, so they can be left whole. As you prepare them, drop them into a bowl of water acidulated with vinegar or lemon juice, so they will not turn black. Clean and trim 500 g (1 lb) of small white onions, leaving them whole, or roughly chop 2 large onions. Wash 2 small lettuces and cut them into strips. Dice 200 g (7 oz) of streaky bacon.

In a heavy-bottomed pan, heat some olive oil and lightly brown the onions and the bacon. Add 10–12 garlic cloves (still in their skins), the drained artichoke bottoms, the strips of lettuce, some pepper and a little salt (but be careful not to add too much salt, because of the bacon). Add a small glass of water. Cover the pan and simmer for an hour. If necessary, add some more water from time to time.

The Countess' Potatoes
~

Imagine an aristocrat from the Alpille Hills, barefooted, sleeves rolled up, skirts tied up in her belt. She is busy around the cooking pots, dishing out food with a smile, seemingly without effort. She is our friend Françoise, the Countess.

IN THE KITCHEN : For this marvellous stew, you need approximately equal quantities of potatoes and other seasonal vegetables, whatever you have on hand. For instance, artichokes, baby onions and broad beans, or carrots, turnips and the white part of leeks, or aubergines, red peppers and tomatoes. With spring vegetables, the potatoes will be new baby potatoes, but with carrots and leeks, for example, you will be using older potatoes, cut into pieces of a similar size to the vegetables. Pertuis potatoes are ideal for this recipe.

Wash and peel the vegetables, then cut them into 4 cm (1½ inch) pieces. In a heavy-bottomed pan, heat 2 or 3 tablespoons of olive oil and lightly brown 2 sliced onions. Add 3 unpeeled garlic cloves, 2 bay leaves, a sprig of thyme, the potatoes and the vegetables, 3 tablespoons of water, salt and freshly ground pepper, to taste. Cover and cook over a low heat for at least 30 minutes. Add a few extra drops of water, if necessary. About 10 minutes before serving, add a bowl of black olives, and lightly stir into the vegetable mixture, to avoid mashing them. Let the olives heat through before serving.

My Strawberry Cake

~

This is the cake I always made every year for Mother's Day. It was a whole morning's work, and it would have been much worse if my mother had not played the role of a young chef's help, by washing and drying plates and spoons and generally cleaning up as I went along. She was invaluable.

I do not remember where or when I discovered this recipe, but it is absolutely delicious and rather spectacular.

IN THE KITCHEN : In a large bowl, beat 4 whole eggs with 2 tablespoons of hot (but not boiling) water. With a wooden spoon stir in 150 g (5 oz) of caster sugar and 1 tablespoon of vanilla sugar, then sift in 100 g (3½ oz) of plain flour, 100 g (3½ oz) of potato flour and 6 g (¼ oz) of baking powder. Stir lightly to mix. Pour the batter into a buttered deep cake tin and bake for 30 minutes in a warm oven. Then turn the cake out on to a wire cooling rack and leave it to cool.

Whip 500 ml (17 fl oz) of double cream until just stiff and sweeten it with a little vanilla sugar, to taste. Using a long-bladed knife, cut the cake horizontally into 3–4 layers, each about 1 cm (½ inch) thick. Spread raspberry jam over the bottom cake layer, cover with slices of fresh strawberries, then with some of the whipped cream. Repeat these layers, finishing with a layer of cake. Cover the whole cake with the remaining whipped cream and decorate with whole strawberries and strawberry leaves and flowers.

Auntie Lilette's Strawberry Cake

~

In our family, we have another strawberry cake to rival the recipe above. It is simpler, lighter, very delicate and just as delicious. So much so, that my family have never been able to agree on which was the best. This is my Aunt Elisabeth's recipe.

IN THE KITCHEN : Crush 200 g (7 oz) of strawberries with a little sugar. Pour this strawberry purée into a plastic tray and place in the freezer. While the sorbet is hardening, weigh 5 eggs in their shells. You require the same weight of sugar and half the weight of potato flour. Separate the eggs. Beat the yolks with the sugar until the mixture is smooth and pale. In a separate bowl, beat the egg whites with a pinch of salt until they hold firm peaks.

Carefully fold the sifted potato flour into the egg yolks, then very lightly fold in the stiff egg whites.

Pour the mixture into a buttered cake tin and bake in a warm oven for 30 minutes. Then turn the cake out on to a wire rack and leave it to cool completely. Cut it in half horizontally and fill it with the strawberry sorbet. Cover the cake completely with whipped cream and decorate with whole strawberries. This cake must be assembled at the very last minute.

Acacia Blossom Fritters

~

You will find acacia trees everywhere in Provence, tall, elegant trees which in April are covered with lovely white blossoms. It is with these that we are going to make our fritters, having taken a basket and gathered some of those beautiful fragrant clusters from the tree, earlier that day.

IN THE KITCHEN : In a bowl, make a batter with 250 g (8 oz) of plain flour, a pinch of salt and 150 ml (¼ pint) of water. Add 1 whole egg and 1 tablespoon of olive oil. Beat the batter with a balloon whisk until it is smooth. Let the batter rest for 1–2 hours. Just before making the fritters, beat 2 egg whites with a pinch of salt until stiff and then fold them lightly into the batter.

Heat some oil in a deep-fat fryer. Dip the acacia blossoms into the batter and then plunge them into the hot oil. Be careful, because the hot fat may spit. Once golden, turn them over, cook on the other side, and then take them out of the fat, using a slotted spoon. Drain the fritters on a piece of kitchen paper. Sprinkle with caster sugar and serve warm.

Acacia Blosso
Fritt•

BREAKFAST WITH THE HORSEMEN

In Camargue, life starts at daybreak. Just enough time to drink a cup of coffee, and then *les gardians* (horsemen) are on their horses. There is not a morning when they do not have to ride over earth or water to muster or separate the herds of bulls. As for me, well, I am not a good horseman, and by nature more contemplative than active. I prefer to stroll around, and I go and 'take the pulse of the lake', watch the birds and float in and out of day-dreams. So, when around 10 o'clock we go back to the house, a little tired, and feeling hungry, what a joy it is for me and *les gardians* to see the table set under the tamarisk trees, and smell the aromas of the meal prepared by the ladies of the house. The dried sausage from Arles and the olives, the salad of cuttlefish with warm potatoes and *aïoli*, the grilled aubergines, the jar of *cachat* (cheese) and the rice pudding. Not to forget the *Carthagène* wine shining in the sun.

The horses of the Camargue grazing on a prairie

Watermelon Jam and 'Carthagène' wine

Broken Olives

~

Olives and the dried sausages from Arles are inseparable companions. The olives are harvested here in September. At that time, the olives are plump, but still green. It is with these olives that you will prepare 'broken' olives. In October, the olives turn purple. At the end of November, they are black and full of oil, so you would then be able to prepare 'pricked' olives. Olive harvesting for oil-making will go on until Saint Blaise's Day, which is at the beginning of February, and there is a local saying that goes: '*Per Santo Catarino, l'oli es à l'oulivo, Per San Blaise, l'es encore mai*' – 'on Saint Catherine's Day, the oil is in the olive, on Saint Blaise's Day, it is there even more'.

IN THE KITCHEN : The first olives, the green ones, harvested in September, are acid and bitter, and before you can eat them, you will have to get rid of this bitterness. Take 1.5 kg (3 lb) of freshly picked green olives, split them one by one with a wooden mallet but do not crush them. Soak the olives in cold water for at least a week, changing the water every day. My friend Annie Laurent does this for a whole month. On the last day, in a pan place 250 g (8 oz) of coarse sea salt, 1 sprig of fennel, a few bay leaves, 3–4 garlic cloves, still in their skins, and a piece of dried orange peel in 3 litres (5 pints) of boiling water. Remove the pan from the heat and let all the flavours infuse in the water until it is completely cold. Drain the olives, place them in a glazed earthenware pot and cover them with the flavoured water. Store the olives in a cool place and wait for at least a week before eating them.

Be careful though, because they will not keep for more than about 2 months.

Pricked Olives

~

Black olives are less bitter than green ones, especially if you can wait for the crop-in-January variety, *les grossanes*, fully ripened, engorged with oil and a little wrinkled. All you need to do then is to prick them several times with a needle.

To speed up the process, my grandmother used to make little 'pricking brushes' by sticking several pins through pieces of cork, and placing us children in charge of this operation. A prick on one side, then the other and then the olive was ready!

Having pricked the olives, you put them into a *tian* or shallow earthenware dish and cover them with fine sea salt to remove any moisture. The following day, rinse them carefully in fresh cold water and place them in a glazed earthenware pot with lots of fresh thyme, a little rosemary, a few bay leaves, 3–4 whole garlic cloves, 1–2 small hot chillies, if you like them, and enough olive oil to cover. You can make large quantities of 'pricked olives' and they will keep until next season without any problem.

'Meissounenco à la Sucarello'

~

At most Provençal markets, you can buy snails, and normally the peasant who is selling them will have already purged them (to cleanse their digestive systems) by starving them for a few days, so you can use them straight away. These snails are of a reasonable size, though they are much smaller than the snails you find in Burgundy, and are delicious barbecued over hot coals or cooked in boiling water flavoured with herbs, and served with an *aïoli* (see recipe on page 184). But to make our *sucarello*, we need the tiny snails which appear in the morning dew and then as soon as the temperature rises, climb to the top of fennel plants, wooden posts or even trees. They are striped yellow and grey and we call them *limaçons* or *meissounenco*. You will not find these at the market. So, pick up a wire basket, go for a morning stroll, and find about a hundred of these colourful dew snails.

IN THE KITCHEN : These snails are so small it is not necessary to purge them, but they do need to soak for about 12 hours in a large bowl filled with water, to which a cup of salt and 250 ml (8 fl oz) of vinegar have been added. At the end of that time, rinse the snails several times in fresh cold water, then pat dry. Now you need a little patience, because the top of the spiral on each shell must be carefully pierced, using a sharp kitchen knife. That way, it will be easier to suck the snails out of their shells, once they are cooked. That is how we eat them, *à la sucarello*.

Cook the snails in a well-flavoured stock with some strips of fennel, a few sprigs of thyme, a bay leaf and a piece of dried orange peel. Boil the snails for 30 minutes, then drain them thoroughly. Prepare a vinaigrette with a little vinegar, olive oil, sea salt and freshly ground pepper. Just before serving pour the vinaigrette over the snails, and sprinkle generously with chopped fresh parsley.

Fisherman's 'Rouille' from Les Marquises

~

Les Marquises is the name of my friends Henri and Annie Laurent's beautiful property, which lies between Lake Vacares and the man-made salt marshes of Giraud. At Annie's table, we enjoy the generous and genuine food of Camargue. Often the meal starts with this marvellous fisherman's *rouille*. In fact, this is a *rouille* in name only. The real *rouille* is a sauce deriving its name from the colour and the flavour of Spanish red peppers and which is used to enhance fish soups, stews and *bouillabaisses* (see recipe on page 130). In this *rouille* there are no peppers, no orange colour, just a small teaspoon of mustard in an *aïoli*, a heresy which might shock traditionalists but which gives, as I have told you, a superb result.

IN THE KITCHEN : This potato salad requires some organization, because it must be served very hot or it will lose all its character. I will give you the proportions for 12 people. First boil 2 kg (4 lb) of potatoes in their skins in a pan of water, with 1 leek, 1 onion, 1 garlic clove, 2 bay leaves, a little thyme and some freshly ground white pepper. Then, prepare 2 kg (4 lb) of cuttlefish, removing

the bones and the ink sacs. Cut the fish into 2.5 cm (1 inch) squares. Prepare a stock with 750 ml (1¼ pints) of water, 250 ml (8 fl oz) of white wine, 1 leek, 1 onion, some slices of lemon, some garlic cloves, some fresh herbs, some sea salt and freshly ground pepper.

Simmer the stock for 15 minutes, then lower the heat and add the pieces of cuttlefish. Continue to cook for about 20 minutes. Meanwhile, prepare an *aïoli*, referring to the recipe on page 184, but adding a teaspoon of Dijon mustard to the garlic and the egg yolk before incorporating the olive oil. Drain the potatoes; while still hot peel and chop them. Drain the cuttlefish, discarding the stock, herbs and vegetables. Mix the potatoes and the fish with the flavoured *aïoli*. Serve this fisherman's *rouille* straight away, while still piping hot. I personally like to present this dish in a warm tureen with a lid.

Tellines à l'aïoli

~

WINE:
Vin de Pays
rosé or
Faugères blanc

A *telline* is a small bivalve shellfish which lives on the sandy beaches of Camargue. You can find them at all the good fishmongers in Provence. First, let the *tellines* soak in fresh water overnight, to get rid of their sand. Then you need to prepare a good *aïoli* with 500 ml (17 fl oz) of oil, using the recipe on page 184. Just before serving, put a small glass of white wine, 1 shallot and 1 garlic clove, both finely chopped, and a drop of olive oil into a large saucepan, and bring to the boil. Add the *tellines,* cover the pan and cook over a high heat for about 5 minutes, shaking the pan from time to time, until they open. Alternatively, simply place the washed *tellines* in a pan and cook until they open, which is almost better. Discard

any shells that remain closed. Let the *tellines* cool slightly, but not too much. Mix them with the *aïoli* and serve warm.

A Picturesque Salad

~

There is another hot potato salad which could be the long-lost twin sister of the fisherman's *rouille*. It is a similar recipe, with the same intense and luxurious flavours, but its origins are far from Camargue – this recipe comes from Luxembourg. It may seem out of place, but never mind!

IN THE KITCHEN : Boil 1 kg (2 lb) of potatoes, still in their skins. In a deep frying pan brown some large cubes of bacon over a low heat. When they are golden, but not dry, lower the heat and add a bowl of fresh single cream, a little wine vinegar and a teaspoon of mustard. The sauce should have a sweet and sour taste. Pepper generously. Poach a few garlic sausages (but do not forget to prick them with a fork to prevent them from bursting) and a few frankfurters in simmering water. Then, cut the sausages into thick slices. Drain the potatoes, then peel and cut them into cubes. Mix the potatoes and the sausages into the cream and bacon sauce and serve immediately. Like the fisherman's *rouille*, this salad should be served hot.

Jérôme's Aubergine Stew

~

My good friend Jérôme is an inspired cook. He explores, experiments, researches and rejuvenates with passion the simplest country recipes, like this one: aubergines cooked like little legs of lamb. It is the easiest and the prettiest of all the aubergine stews I know.

IN THE KITCHEN : Prepare the aubergines: wash and dry, top and tail, but do not peel them. Take about 20 peeled garlic cloves and split them in half lengthways. At regular intervals, about every 1 cm (½ inch), insert a piece of garlic into the aubergines – as you would for a leg of lamb. Pour a little olive oil into a heavy-bottomed pan and add the aubergines. Season with sea salt and freshly ground pepper. Cover and cook over a low heat for a good hour.

Grilled Peppers
and Aubergines

~

Prepare a dressing with a little extra-virgin olive oil, sea salt, freshly ground pepper and parsley and garlic, both finely chopped.

Light a fire of vine shoots, and place a griddle over it, positioned high enough so that the flames barely touch it.

Wash and dry some aubergines and red peppers without peeling or tailing them. Prick the aubergines to prevent them bursting and grill the vegetables over the flames. They will turn completely black but do not worry about this. Turn them over frequently so they will cook evenly on all sides.

When they are ready, peel the aubergines but do not take off the stems. Peel, seed and cut the peppers into strips. Arrange the vegetables on a serving dish and pour the dressing over them.

You can also bake the vegetables in the oven and serve them in the same way, but you will miss out on the delicious smoky flavour – which makes all the difference – that grilling over a wood fire imparts to the vegetables.

'Lou Cachat'

~

Lou cachat is a deliciously strong, slightly pungent cheese mixture which is an ideal way of using up all the leftover bits of cheese that have dried out.

To make a good cachat, just like a good vinegar, you need a 'mother', which you will be able to get from a generous friend who has a pot of cachat in their cellar, and will be ready to give you some. So, once you have been given a bowlful of cachat, take a large stoneware pot with a lid. Put your cachat 'mother' into it with all your leftover bits of cheese, mashed by hand or in a food processor. Pour a little white alcohol over the top. Mix, then cover the pot and leave it for at least a month before tasting it. Whenever you have some left-over cheese, add it to the cheese and alcohol mixture, topping up with alcohol when necessary.

WINE:
Châteauneuf
du Pape
blanc

Grilled
Peppers and
Aubergines

Annie Laurent's
Rice Pudding
~

First, you need to make a dark golden caramel (see recipe on page 41) using 20 sugar cubes and a little water – just enough to moisten the sugar. Take care not to burn the caramel or it will taste bitter. When it is golden brown but still liquid, remove from the heat and pour it into an ovenproof dish; turn and tilt the dish so the caramel coats the sides of the dish, then leave it to cool.

Cook 1 cupful of Camargue round rice (short-grain rice), washed and drained, in a pan of boiling water for 5 minutes. In another pan, bring 1 litre (1¾ pints) of milk to the boil with a split vanilla pod and 3 or 4 pieces of dried orange peel. When the milk starts boiling, lower the heat and add the drained rice. Cook for an hour over a low heat until the milk is almost completely absorbed. The rice must still be creamy. Take the pan off the heat. Beat 4 whole eggs with a little caster sugar, but not too much because the caramel will also sweeten the pudding. Stir the rice into the eggs, remove the vanilla pod but leave the orange peel. At

this point, you can add glacé fruit and sultanas, but they are optional, not essential. Pour the rice mixture into the caramelized dish and cook in a bain-marie in a warm oven for 30–40 minutes. Let the pudding cool completely before turning it out on to a serving dish. This pudding tastes even better when it is a day old.

Watermelon Jam

~

In Provence, we use a special watermelon for jam, it is oblong, a pale green colour with even paler flesh. We call it *la meraviho*, the 'marvel'. Do not use the round watermelon with a dark rind and red flesh studded with black pips. This melon is only good eaten raw, when it is ripe and sweet.

IN THE KITCHEN : The day before, cut the watermelon into slices, remove the rind and pips and dice the flesh. Then, weigh it. For each 1 kg (2 lb) of fruit, add 1 unwaxed lemon (sliced finely), a split vanilla pod and 750 g (1½ lb) of granulated or caster sugar. Let all this marinate overnight.

The following day, put the fruit mixture into a preserving pan and cook for 30 minutes. Repeat this for three consecutive days until the fruit is translucent and the syrup thick. Let the jam cool, and then pour into sterilized jars. Keep an eye on the jam when cooking it, because it has a tendency to foam and could easily boil over.

Like fig jam (see page 165) and green tomato jam (see page 33), this is a perfect dessert jam, to be served with biscuits or fresh cheese.

'Carthagène'

~

In Provençal, we say *Cartagèno*. This drink is a beautiful deep amber colour and is frequently served as an aperitif or as a dessert wine. Historically *Carthagène* was a royal drink and in Arles it traditionally accompanies the 13 desserts served on Christmas Eve.

If you are offered some *Carthagène* in the Camargue, consider it an honour.

IN THE KITCHEN : At grape-picking time, mix 3 litres (5 pints) of fresh white grape juice with 1 litre (1¾ pints) of new grape alcohol (about 60° proof). Let the mixture ferment at least until All Saints' Day (1st November), then store it in a cold cellar for a year . . . Then filter, bottle, seal and label each bottle. *Carthagène* wine improves with age.

BOUILLABAISSE IN AN ARTIST'S STUDIO

There is THE *bouillabaisse*, which is made with fish, and then there are all the other varieties which use eggs, spinach, sardines, green peas, salt cod and goodness knows what else. They are not as famous, but they are always delicious served with toasted bread and grated cheese which melts in the hot soup. The variations are more common inland where people could not get fish or were too poor to buy it. They smell beautifully of fennel and saffron, but they have nothing in common with true *bouillabaisse*.

The name comes from the Provençal words *boui-abaisso*, meaning, in the words of Frédéric Mistral, the Provençal poet: '*boui*, the pot is boiling, *abaisso*, turn the heat down, because you only need a little simmering to cook this dish'. There is another explanation for the name, which describes the squatting (*abaissée*) position of the fishermen around the wood fire on which the pot is boiling, because in the olden days, this peasant soup was prepared on the beach.

But today, thanks to the marvels of refrigerated transport, you can find fresh fish everywhere in Provence so that you can make *bouillabaisse* anywhere. And so, I invite you to a painter's lunch to taste his special recipe.

The table is set by a window overlooking the garden. Everywhere large canvasses are stacked up or set up on easels. A large trolley covered with pots and brushes will serve as a side-table for piles of plates and napkins. Everything, the cooking and the eating, will take place in the studio. For the occasion we will give up working with paints to

rinks in
érard Drouillet's
udio in
ygalières

123

concentrate on the *bouillabaisse*, we will exchange the brush for the wooden spoon, and the fish will marinate alongside tubes and pots of paint. Meanwhile, we will have a drink of *pastis* or chilled white wine from Cassis, and we will nibble on *poutargue* or anchovy toast, or on little fried ravioli the way Françoise makes them. The subtle aroma of saffron mingles with the fennel, garlic and fresh fish. The *bouillabaisse* is almost ready and the rockfish soup is already steaming in the strange soup bowl from Vallauris, a glazed bowl in the shape of a *rascasse* with elegantly made-up doe eyes. Next to a plaster Hercules a magnificent bowl of snow cream is waiting near a plate of homemade biscuits which we will eat later on . . .

But we are still enjoying our drinks and we have had to toast a basketful of thin slices of bread. The toast will be spread with solidified olive oil and grated *poutargue* or tapenade (olive paste), or with the poor man's sauce (made with anchovies and almonds).

Solidified Olive Oil
and Grated Poutargue

~

Poutargue is the caviar of Provence. It is the eggs of the grey mullet which used to come and breed in Lake Berre. Unfortunately, there are no grey mullet left in Lake Berre, so no more real *poutargue* in Martigues. But you can get *poutargue* from North Africa, not as good, old people will tell you, but still delicious. The fish eggs, still in their original pouch, are salted, then pressed and dried. These days, they are covered with a thin film of wax or paraffin.

IN THE KITCHEN : Remove the layer of wax and the thin skin which protects the eggs. Then grate them using a Parmesan grater.

The day before, or at least a few hours before, you will have filled a bowl with fruity extra-virgin olive oil. Put this bowl in the freezer so that the oil will solidify. When ready, spread it on thin slices of toast, as you would butter, and sprinkle generously with the grated *poutargue*. Eat it quickly before the oil melts.

Black Tapenade

~

Whether it is black or green, tapenade does not take its name from the olive, which is nevertheless the main ingredient, but from the caper – *tapeno* in Provençal. So strictly speaking, it is a caper spread.

To make black tapenade you should use the black olives from Nyons.

IN THE KITCHEN : Stone 300 g (10 oz) of black olives and chop them finely. Put them in a mortar with 12 anchovy fillets, which have been rinsed in fresh water, and a large tablespoon of capers. Mash all the ingredients together thoroughly with a wooden pestle. Add a dash of olive oil and a few drops of lemon juice. You will need 1 anchovy fillet and 3 capers for every 10 olives. Serve with toasted bread.

Some people grind pepper into their tapenade, and that is not a bad idea.

Other people replace the lemon juice in the basic tapenade recipe with 1 tablespoon of rum. I personally prefer the lemon juice.

Others also add half a mashed garlic clove. It is simply a question of how you like your tapenade to taste.

Green Tapenade
~

Take 250 g (8 oz) of stoned green olives, finely chopped, and 100 g (3½ oz) of blanched almonds. Using a pestle and mortar, mash the nuts and the olives together with 1 large tablespoon of capers, 6 anchovy fillets, a dash of olive oil and, why not, if you like, add a dash of old marc brandy.

Anchovy Quichets
~

Wash 6 large anchovies under running water and then fillet them. Using a pestle and mortar, mash them with 1 garlic clove and a little olive oil. Spread this paste on small thin slices of bread and grill these *quichets* (toasts) lightly in a hot oven for 5 minutes. Serve warm.

Almond and Garlic Sauce
~

Using a pestle and mortar, crush about 30 blanched almonds with 5 garlic cloves. Add a few drops of water, then little by little add some olive oil until the paste has thickened and is smooth. Serve on toasted bread.

Almond and Anchovy Sauce

~

Frédéric Mistral used to call this the poor man's sauce, because a small piece of bread spread with this paste would make a complete meal.

Using a pestle and mortar, mash about 30 almonds or walnut kernels with a few anchovy fillets and some sprigs of fennel. Add a few drops of water, then some olive oil until the paste is thick and smooth. Serve with toast or batons of raw vegetables, such as carrots, celery, fennel bulb, cauliflower, as for the *anchoïade* sauce (see recipe on page 141).

Fried Ravioli

~

Buy some little ravioli like those made in the town of Romans – tiny ones filled with *brousse* cheese. They are generally poached for a few seconds in chicken stock, but my friend, Françoise, when she invites us to her beautiful château in the Alpille Hills, likes to serve them fried, as a snack with drinks.

IN THE KITCHEN : Separate the ravioli carefully and fry them in a pan in 1 cm (½ inch) of hot, but not smoking, olive oil, just long enough to give them a nice golden colour. Remove the ravioli with a slotted spoon and drain on a piece of kitchen paper. Then salt them generously and serve them straight away, piping hot.

Bouillabaisse from the Villepontoux Restaurant

~

WINE:
Cassis
blanc

There is not one, but a thousand ways of making *bouillabaisse*. Some people add leeks. Others add potatoes. Each area, each family even, has its own secret recipe.

In Marseilles, on the old coast road – old *Marseillais* will remember it – there was a restaurant right in the middle of Prophet's Bay – Le Villepontoux. It was the restaurant owned by Elie and Jeanne Drouillet, my friend Gérard Drouillet's parents. They used to serve a *bouillabaisse* famous throughout the district and even farther. I have often eaten this *bouillabaisse* at the table of my friend 'Queen Jeanne' and it is unbeatable. It is this *bouillabaisse* recipe that I am going to share with you now. There are 3 stages and this recipe will serve about 6 people.

IN THE KITCHEN : *La soupe de poissons de roche* (rockfish soup).

First, you make a delicious soup with *poissons de roche*. In a large saucepan, heat 1 tablespoon of olive oil and cook the flesh of 2 large tomatoes for about 5 minutes with 2 sprigs of fennel, a bay leaf, 2 peeled and lightly crushed garlic cloves, a piece of dried orange peel, some saffron, salt and pepper. Add 1.5 kg (3 lb) of *poissons de roche*. These are small Mediterranean fish of various species that live among the rocks along the coast. There is no precise equivalent outside France, but you could always use a mixture of fresh fish and shellfish, including halibut, red snapper, scallops and clams. *Poissons de roche* are used whole and do not need cleaning. Cover with 2 litres (3½ pints) of cold water, bring to the boil, then lower the heat and simmer for 45 minutes. Strain the soup through a fine sieve, pressing well on the fish to extract all the juices.

If you are serving this soup on its own, pour it into warmed soup bowls and serve with garlic croûtons, grated cheese and *rouille* sauce or sea urchin *rouille*.

The *bouillabaisse*:
To continue with the *bouillabaisse*, you will need really fresh fish:
— 6 monkfish steaks
— 6 conger eel steaks
— 3 weevers
— 1 John Dory
— 4 scorpion fish, the famous *rascasse*
You can also add white scorpion fish, or some gurnards.
Clean and scale all the fish, reserving their livers. Now we are going to make a

*Marinating t...
bouillabais...*

marinade, and this is undoubtedly the secret of this particular recipe. Place all the fish in a large dish with some sprigs of fennel, some tomatoes and potatoes, both peeled and sliced, some sea salt, freshly ground pepper and saffron. Pour over a little olive oil, mix well and let the fish marinate for a few hours in a cool place. Bring the rockfish soup to the boil. As soon as it starts boiling, add the potatoes with all the marinade, but not the fish. Return to the boil, lower the heat and simmer for 10 minutes. Then add the firm-fleshed fish: the monkfish, the scorpion fish and the conger eel. After 10 more minutes, lower the heat, and add the soft-fleshed fish: the John Dory and the weever. Cook for a further 5 minutes. Taste and adjust the seasoning as required. As a first course, serve the soup with garlic croûtons, grated cheese and sea urchin *rouille*. As a second course, serve the fish with the potatoes, a blob of sea urchin *rouille*, and some more soup to moisten the fish.

The *rouille*:

This owes its name to the colour given to it by the red peppers from Spain. Using a pestle and mortar, mash 3 garlic cloves and 3 chopped Spanish red peppers. Add a walnut-sized piece of bread, which you have moistened with fish soup, then squeezed dry. When the bread is blended into the garlic and pepper paste, slowly beat in some olive oil, a drop at a time, until the sauce thickens. When the *rouille* is thick and firm, like a mayonnaise, you can serve it as it is, or add a small ladle of stock from the *bouillabaisse* and present it in a sauce-boat.

Sea urchin *rouille*:

Sea urchin *rouille* is not as strong in flavour as traditional *rouille*, and I think it is delicious. You will need about 5 tablespoons of sea urchin coral. First, plunge the reserved fish livers into the hot soup for 2 minutes and then drain them well. Now, using a pestle and mortar, mash 3 garlic cloves with the fish livers. Add 1 egg yolk (which has been kept at room temperature), a pinch of sea salt, some freshly ground pepper, a few strands of saffron and the sea urchin coral. Gradually beat in the olive oil, a little at a time, to thicken the sauce in the same way as you would for mayonnaise.

Fishermen's Bouillabaisse

~

This is a much simpler *bouill-abaisse*, but just as authentic, and perfect to be eaten at the beach house. The flavourings are the same, except for saffron which is not used in this recipe (too expensive). The fish will be chosen, depending on the catch of the day, from the following: red and white scorpion fish, gurnards, conger eel, John Dory, weevers, monkfish, sea bass and even crabs and small crayfish.

Clean and scale the fish. Cut them into large pieces, and marinate them for 30 minutes in a large pot with some strips of fennel, a bay leaf, a piece of dried orange peel, 1 garlic clove (crushed), the flesh of a tomato, a leek and an onion (both roughly chopped), some sea salt, freshly ground pepper and a little olive oil. Meanwhile, heat 3 litres (5 pints) of water and simmer the fish which are too small to use, with the heads from the larger fish. Place the pot containing the marinade over a medium heat, and pour over the drained fish stock. Bring it back to the boil, lower the heat and simmer for about 10 minutes. It is now ready to eat.

Salt Cod Bouillabaisse

~

Soak the salt cod for 24 hours, changing the water frequently. Then poach the cod by placing it in a pan of cold water. As soon as the water starts to boil, remove the pan from the heat. Leave it to poach for about 10 minutes, then drain it, reserving the cooking water. Skin and bone the fish.

In a pot, brown 2 finely chopped onions in a little olive oil. Then add the flesh of 2-3 tomatoes (which has been pressed through a sieve), 6 chopped garlic cloves, a few sprigs of fennel, 2 bay leaves, a piece of dried orange peel, a little thyme, a little parsley and some freshly ground pepper. Mix all these ingredients together with a wooden spoon and add 5-6 thickly sliced potatoes. Cover with the reserved poaching water, and cook over a high heat for about 30 minutes. When the potatoes are tender, lower the heat and add the pieces of cod, just long enough to heat them through, together with a few strands of saffron. Saffron preserves its flavour better if it is not cooked.

Place the warmed soup plates on the table. Serve the fish and potatoes in a dish and the stock in a warmed soup tureen, accompanied by a bowl of *aïoli* (see recipe on page 184), a bowl of grated cheese, and some garlic toast.

WINE: Bandol rosé

One-eyed Bouillabaisse

~

Finely slice 2 leeks and 1 onion. In a heavy-bottomed pan heat 1 tablespoon of olive oil and brown the leeks and onion. Add the finely chopped flesh of 3 tomatoes, 4 chopped garlic cloves, a few sprigs of fennel, 2 bay leaves and a piece of dried orange peel, some sea salt and some freshly ground pepper. Add 6-7 thickly sliced potatoes and cover the pan. Cook over a fairly high heat until the potatoes are tender, then lower the heat so the stock barely simmers. Add a few strands of saffron. Then, allowing 1 egg per person, break each egg into a cup and one by one gently drop them into the stock. Allow to poach for a few minutes.

Serve in warmed soup bowls on large slices of toasted bread sprinkled with grated cheese.

Stuffed 'Capon'

~

I got this recipe from a fisherman in Sainte-Maxime. In this part of the world, a *chapon* (capon) is not the large fowl that we roast for Christmas, it is a beautiful red fish, a type of large *rascasse*. Ask your fishmonger to fillet the fish through the back. He will have to open up the fish along the dorsal fin, sliding his knife along both sides of the backbone, and snapping it at the base of the head to allow it to be removed, along with the guts. Then prepare the stuffing: finely chop 300 g (10 oz) of white fish, 300 g (10 oz) of cooked ham, 100 g (3½ oz) of stoned black olives and 1 garlic clove.

Add a little olive oil, a pinch of salt – but sparingly because the ham and the olives are already salted – and some freshly ground pepper. Bind with an egg yolk and mix well.

Stuff the fish with this mixture and tie it up with kitchen string so that it will keep its round shape. Insert bay leaves between the string and the fish, place it in a baking dish and drizzle a couple of tablespoons of olive oil over it. Bake it in a moderate oven for about 1¼ hours, maybe longer depending on the size of the fish. The stuffing must be cooked through. Baste from time to time during cooking, and serve hot.

WINE: Cassis blanc

Snow Cream

~

For the snow cream (floating islands) we are going to make a custard with 8 eggs and 1 litre (1¾ pints) of milk. Separate the whites from the yolks, keeping only 5 egg whites.

In a bowl, beat the yolks with 100 g (3½ oz) of caster sugar until the mixture is smooth and pale.

In a pan, heat the milk. Beat the egg whites with a pinch of salt until very stiff, and then poach tablespoons of egg white, a few at a time, in the simmering milk, until they are set, about 2 minutes on each side. Remove with a slotted spoon and drain well. Place them in a pretty serving dish.

Make a caramel with 20 sugar cubes (see recipe on page 41). Pour one-third of the caramel on to the poached egg whites.

Strain the milk and mix with the

Pages 134–135:
Crunchy Almond Biscuits,
Shortbread, Rock Biscuits
and Snow Cream

remaining caramel. Then, stirring constantly, very gradually pour the hot milk on to the yolk and sugar mixture. Return the mixture to a cleaned pan and place the pan over a very low heat; cook the custard, stirring constantly, until it thickens slightly. Do not let it boil or the custard will curdle.

Pour the custard into the dish around the floating islands, and let it cool. Chill in the refrigerator for an hour before serving.

Rock Biscuits

In a large bowl, mix 250 g (8 oz) of caster sugar, 1 tablespoon of vanilla sugar, and 125 g (4 oz) of softened butter. Add 500 g (1 lb) of flour all at once and mix well. In another bowl, whisk 1 cup of milk with 1 whole egg and 1 teaspoon of bicarbonate of soda. Slowly add the milk to the flour and sugar mixture and blend without working the dough too much – it should stay lumpy. Drop little heaps of dough on to buttered baking sheets, and cook these little rocks for 15–20 minutes in a moderate oven.

Shortbread

In a bowl, mix 200 g (7 oz) of flour, 125 g (4 oz) of sugar, 1 egg, 1 teaspoon of baking powder, 3 tablespoons of milk, 100 g (3½ oz) of melted butter, and the grated rind of an orange. Mix quickly, and roll the dough out until it is 5 mm (¼ inch) thick. With a glass, cut out rounds of dough. Place these on buttered baking sheets, brush with milk and cook for 15 minutes in a moderate oven.

Crunchy
Almond Biscuits
~

Provençal grandmothers know how to make two kinds of pale golden biscuits. There are those you serve in the drawing room with a glass of muscat wine, biscuits for 'when we have guests', like the *navettes* (see page 163) or short-bread biscuits, and those for the children for afternoon tea or dessert, like crunchy almond biscuits or rock biscuits. We used to call these crunchy almond biscuits tooth-breakers, and as a matter of fact, they are extremely hard, but try dipping them in a glass of wine. . .

IN THE KITCHEN : First, make a syrup with 325 g (11 oz) of sugar and 100 ml (3½ fl oz) of water. Let it cook slowly, stirring constantly until it reaches the *filet* stage (see page 31). Take the pan off the heat, pour the syrup into a large bowl and stir in 325 g (11 oz) of blanched almonds. Let them soak in the syrup for 4 hours. At the end of that time, carefully place 500 g (1 lb) of flour on to a smooth surface – a marble slab would be ideal. Make a well in the centre of the flour and pour in the syrup with the almonds. Add 4 whole eggs and a pinch of salt. Work the dough first with your fingertips, then knead it lightly until it is smooth. Roll it out until it is 1 cm (½ inch) thick, then cut it into strips 20 cm (8 inches) long by 3 cm (1¼ inches) wide. Place the strips on a buttered baking sheet and bake them for 20 minutes in a moderate oven. Remove from the oven, and a few minutes later, when they have cooled slightly, cut them up into smaller strips measuring 1 x 3 cm (½ x 1¼ inches). Leave them to cool completely and store in an airtight tin.

A Picnic on the Banks
of the River Sorgue

Springing from the rocks at Fontaine-de-Vaucluse, the River Sorgue flows, fresh and clear, through the Comtat plain, then divides into several streams around l'Isle-sur-la-Sorgue. The magic starts where the streams appear. The sun bursts out and its rays penetrate the deep shade of the large plane trees to speckle the waters of the Sorgue streams. There, beside the clear water, in the soft magic of the trees, we often go and have lunch on the grass. Every picnic starts with a large basket. We have never had one of those splendid wicker picnic hampers that one can admire in the Manufrance catalogue: large compartments stacked with china secured with leather straps, with forks on one side and knives on the other, bottles encased in wicker holders and even a small portable stove in an enamel tin. We have never owned such a treasure. We use a large basket with one handle, so heavy when laden that we need two people to carry it. In it, we pack the tablecloth and the napkins, the china and the cutlery, the bottles of wine and water and the food.

A picnic is a time to totally escape from the normal family routine: no dining room, no set places at the table and hands, rather than forks, are used to pick up the food. Even when a column of ants marches across the tablecloth, we sit back, slightly bemused, and watch them walk on by.

Nevertheless, a picnic has its own rituals. For example, the menu is always the same: a cold tomato omelette or an *anchoïade* dip to start with, then a terrine of rabbit or beef in jelly, a noodle salad, a few goats' cheeses for the grown-ups and a box of *Vache-Qui-Rit* (the laughing cow) cheese spread for the children, then for dessert a tart and some fruit, or a cherry clafoutis in the spring.

nchoïade

The Irreplaceable
Tomato Omelette

~

To make a tomato omelette, you need a concentrated *coulis*. The tomato *coulis* is one of the key sauces in Provençal cooking. This Provençal word, which has been integrated into the French cooking vocabulary, means 'liquid purée'. It is used to refer to either a plain tomato preserve, without any seasoning, which replaces fresh tomatoes when they are out of season (see recipe on page 159) or a tomato sauce cooked in olive oil and flavoured with onions or garlic, thyme or basil, black pepper or chillies. There is not one but thousands of recipes, each one for a different use.

IN THE KITCHEN : In 1 tablespoon of olive oil, soften 2–3 finely chopped onions without browning them. Add a few very ripe, well-flavoured tomatoes, washed, dried and seeded, then cut into large pieces. Add 2 finely chopped garlic cloves, a little parsley, a little basil, a little thyme, a pinch of sea salt, some freshly ground pepper and 1 sugar lump. Cover and cook over a very low heat for at least 2 hours. You need to stir the *coulis* from time to time so that it will not catch on

An omelet flipper

the base of the pan. When it has reduced and is a nice deep red colour, you can make the omelette.

Beat 8 eggs lightly – without making them froth – and then stir in a pinch of sea salt, some freshly ground pepper and 5–6 tablespoons of the *coulis*. If you are cooking for a lot of people you will need to make 2 omelettes. Cook the omelette in a frying pan with a little olive oil over a medium heat. When it is cooked on one side, flip it over – either by sliding it on to a large saucepan lid or, if you have one, on to an omelette flipper – and cook the other side. Allow the omelette to cool.

L'anchoïade

~

L'anchoïade is an anchovy sauce. Use anchovies that have been preserved in salt, wash them under cold running water and fillet them; about 10 anchovies will be enough for this sauce. Mash the anchovy fillets with a fork and place them in a frying pan with 1 small glass of olive oil, 1 tablespoon of vinegar and some freshly ground pepper. Some people add garlic to this sauce but I find it alters the taste of the anchovies. Cook the sauce over a very low heat so the anchovies slowly dissolve in the oil without ever boiling. This will take about 15 minutes – do remember to stir constantly.

At home, this sauce is served hot with batons of raw vegetables. For the picnic, it will be transported cold in a screw-top jar. It is delicious with carrots, spring onions, celery, fennel (choose the rounder female bulbs, which are more tender than the male ones) or cauliflower.

Rabbit Terrine

~

First, you will have to bone a large rabbit, leaving the pieces of meat as large as possible. Marinate the meat for at least 3 hours with a small glass of cognac, some fresh tarragon, some sea salt and freshly ground pepper. Then drain the meat carefully, reserving the marinade.

Meanwhile, mince together 625 g (1¼ lb) of pork, 625 g (1¼ lb) of veal and 250 g (8 oz) of streaky bacon. Season with a little fresh tarragon, sea salt and freshly ground pepper. Add the juice from the marinade. Bind the meats with 1 egg yolk.

Line the base and sides of a deep terrine dish with thin, wide slices of pork fat or streaky bacon. Cover with a layer of minced meats, then a layer of rabbit, alternating the layers until the terrine is full. End with a layer of the minced meats.

Cover the top with some more pork fat or streaky bacon and make a hole in the centre. Cover with the lid and bake in a bain-marie in a hot oven for about 1½ hours. When the terrine is cooked, take it out of the oven, remove the lid and

*Pages 142–143:
An island in the
River Sorgue*

weigh the meat down with a little wooden board and a weight of about 250 g (8 oz) – or a can. This will make the pâté set with a good, firm texture. This terrine will keep in the refrigerator for 2–3 months, but you will have to cover it with a 1 cm (½ inch) layer of lard. Anyway, it is better after a few days.

Rabbit Sausage
with Olives
~

To make this delicious sausage, finely mince 400 g (13 oz) of veal and 400 g (13 oz) of pork with 150 g (5 oz) of bacon, 300 g (10 oz) of stoned black olives and 3 garlic cloves. Bone a 1.5 kg (3 lb) rabbit and dice the meat. Combine the rabbit meat with the olive mixture and add 1 small glass of cognac, 2 tablespoons of olive oil, some sea salt and freshly ground pepper (do not be mean with the salt and freshly ground pepper – this sausage needs to be well seasoned). Let the mixture stand for 2 hours. Then bind with 2 whole beaten eggs.

Sew a piece of cloth into a 15 x 50 cm (6 x 20 inch) bag and fill it with the meat mixture. Make sure the meat is firmly packed and sew up the opening. In a fish pan or a large cooking pot, make a stock with just enough water to cover the rabbit sausage, some coarse salt, a few pepper-corns, a bouquet garni (made with the green part of a leek, some bay leaves, a sprig of thyme, a stick of celery, a sprig of parsley and a little sage), 2 carrots, 1 onion studded with 3 cloves and a split calf's foot for the jelly. Put the rabbit sausage in when the stock starts boiling, then lower the heat and simmer gently for 3 hours. Remove the sausage from the stock and let it cool completely before taking it out of the cloth bag. Scoop out the vegetables and herbs and let the broth reduce for a little longer with the calf's foot. Strain the stock and leave it in a cool place to let it set.

Serve the rabbit sausage sliced and gar-nished with cubes of jelly and black olives.

WINE:
Côtes
du Ventoux
rosé

Olive Bread

~

This olive bread, perfect for a picnic, is also delicious served as an *hors d'oeuvre* with an aperitif.

In a bowl, mix in the following order, 300 g (10 oz) of flour, 2 teaspoons of baking powder, ½ teaspoon of fine salt, 150 g (5 oz) of stoned green olives, 150 g (5 oz) of diced ham, 150 g (5 oz) of grated Gruyère cheese, 3 whole eggs, 200 ml (7 fl oz) of Muscat de Beaumes-de-Venise wine and 150 ml (¼ pint) of olive oil. Line a rectangular cake tin with buttered nonstick baking paper. Pour the batter into the tin and bake it in a fairly slow oven for 45 minutes. The bread is cooked when a knife blade inserted in the centre comes out clean. Unlike the fruit cake on page 50, this olive bread is best eaten fresh on the day it is made. But let it cool before you serve it! You should get about 10 slices of olive bread from this recipe.

Chilling the wine in the river

Beef Daube
in Jelly

~

Cut 2 kg (4 lb) of *galinette* into large cubes, the size of an egg (this charming and efficient geometry comes straight from my grandmother Athalie's recipe notebook). *Galinette* is the regional name for beef shin.

On the base of the *daubière*, or cooking pot, place a few pieces of pork rind, a few cubes of streaky bacon, a knob of butter and 1 tablespoon of olive oil, then the pieces of beef shin and a calf's foot, split in half, a sliced carrot, a few pieces of dried orange peel and a bay leaf, and 3 or 4 garlic cloves, peeled and quartered. Season with sea salt (but not too much, because of the bacon) and freshly ground pepper. Pour over a good dry white wine until the meat is immersed. Cover the pan and simmer over a very low heat for 5 hours.

When the *daube* is cooked, remove the pieces of meat and set aside. Strain the juices and skim all the fat carefully.

Pour 2 ladles of the cooking juices into a deep terrine dish. Place the terrine in the freezer for a few minutes to allow the juices to set into a jelly. Arrange the meat on top of the layer of jelly, then pour in the rest of the juices. Cover with a piece of aluminium foil and put the terrine in the refrigerator for a few hours so the jelly will set.

Lumache Pasta Salad
~

One day we were going on a picnic and I did not have much time to prepare the lunch basket, so I improvised and created this delicious and rather rustic salad with the leftovers from the refrigerator and the cupboard. From the day before, I had a *tian* of chickpeas and some green beans. I added half a packet of cooked pasta shells, the ones we call 'elbows' (*lumache*) in Provence, and a few tomatoes. This cold salad was such a success that it is now *de rigueur* every time we have a picnic.

IN THE KITCHEN : You will need lots of fruity extra-virgin olive oil in which you will mix 1 teaspoon of Dijon mustard and 2 tablespoons of wine vinegar. Add a small white onion or a few spring onions, finely chopped, 250 g (8 oz) of *lumache* pasta (cooked *al dente*), 250 g (8 oz) of cooked green beans (they should still be crunchy) and 250 g (8 oz) of cooked chickpeas. (They should have been soaked the night before and cooked for 2 hours in salted water, unless you happen to have on hand some spinach cooking liquid – see page 74. In that case, it would not be necessary to soak them and 1 hour of cooking time would be enough.) Add 250 g (8 oz) of firm tomatoes, washed, dried and quartered, a few capers and finally, a few curls of dry goats' cheese. Leave all these ingredients piled up in your salad bowl. Cover with foil for the trip.

Just before serving, mix the salad.

*Lumache
Pasta Salad*

Beef Daube

~

If you would like a winter *daube*, nice and hot and served with fresh pasta or brown rice from Camargue, the recipe is almost the same as for the beef *daube* in jelly (see recipe on page 145). Use beef cheek instead of shin. Omit the calf's foot, which was only there for the jelly, add 6 or 7 unpeeled garlic cloves instead of the chopped garlic and halve the quantity of white wine. Everything else is the same! One more delightful piece of advice from my grandmother: 'If you want a more economical and more abundant dish, 45 minutes before serving, cut some carrots into thick slices and cook them in boiling salted water with a garlic clove and an onion. At the last minute, add the carrots (discarding the onion and garlic) to the *daube*, along with some black olives. Mix well.'

Nanie's Cake

~

Here is a recipe from my mother, a cake for when you want something quick to make for tea or a picnic.

For each large egg you need 6 tablespoons of plain flour, 6 tablespoons of caster sugar, 4 tablespoons of milk and 4 tablespoons of melted butter, ½ teaspoon of baking powder, and the grated rind of 2 lemons for flavour. A 4-egg quantity would work well.

Mix all these ingredients together in a bowl. Pour the batter into a buttered deep cake tin, and bake for 20 minutes in a moderate oven.

Cherry Clafoutis

~

I love this delicious *clafoutis*, which is made with dark ripe cherries, but you can make it with other kinds of fruit at different times of the year (peaches in summer, pears and figs in autumn, or apples in winter).

Liberally butter a porcelain or earthenware dish, then add enough cherries, tailed but not stoned, to make a layer about 3 cm (1¼ inches) deep. In a separate bowl, mix 5 tablespoons of flour with 5 tablespoons of caster sugar and a pinch of salt. Add 50 ml (2 fl oz) of milk, little by little, whisking well all the time to avoid lumps. Add 5 whole eggs, one at a time. Pour the mixture over the fruit and cook for 15 minutes in a moderate oven. Then take the dish out of the oven and sprinkle the *clafoutis* with caster sugar and dabs of butter. Put the *clafoutis* back in the oven for a further 10 minutes. Serve warm or cold.

A Day at the 'Cabanon'

Our *cabanon* (cabin) is beside a creek, very close to Marseilles. Early in the morning, before catching the boat at *le Vieux-Port*, the Old Harbour, you will need to buy some fish, unless you are absolutely sure you are going to catch your own. We climb on board the boat, loaded like donkeys with food and bottles of water and wine. After the 15-minute boat ride, we have to walk along a stony path laden with our heavy baskets. Finally we arrive at the *cabanon*, the rocks, the sea, the beauty and the freedom of it all!

While some of us are fishing for sea urchins, others are getting the coals ready and Auntie Anne is making the sauce for the pasta. Auntie Anne is a genuine *Marseillaise*, a girl from the Saint-Jean neighbourhood (here, we say a *San Janenque*). She is the grand-daughter of a fishwife from *le Vieux-Port* who, one day, stepped off the boat from Naples and stayed. And that is why the cooking of Marseilles sometimes has an Italian flavour, or so we say in our family. Two years ago, at the Christmas *santon* fair, at the top of the Canebière in Marseilles, a new *santon* figurine made an appearance. Alongside the ox and the donkey, Grasset and Grasseto, the blird man and the pistachio seller, was the *pizzaiolo*, a Neapolitan immigrant who had at last become a true Provençal. This is only fair, since pizza has been a national dish of Provence for such a long time now.

But back to the *cabanon*. The coals are almost ready and the sea bream is patiently wait-ing on its griddle. Deep inside the cooking pot, *le monstre* (octopus) is gurgling among the steam from the garlic and tomato. On the terrace, the children are laying the table.

Spaghetti 'au monstre' in the shade of the cabanon

Talking about the table, this one is a very peculiar construction of boards and marbled vinyl tiles with two rather strange matching chairs. There is an actual style of *cabanon* furniture, one could almost call it *cabanon* art, made of oil cans and broken plates, masses of ingenuity and incredible audacity when it comes to taste! In the *calanques* (creeks) of Cassis, from Goudes to *la pointe Rouge*, around Malmousque, in the *vallon des Auffes*, from Estaque to Martigues and all around Lake Berre, hundreds of *cabanons* bear witness to the fabulous creativity of their builders. There, in a stony environment, with sparse vegetation due to lack of fresh water and the salty vapours of the sea, they have erected these amazing shacks, often made from rubbish collected from the nearby city. But whether they have been prettily arranged or stand proud in their plainness, all of them in their simplicity or their folly are dedicated to pleasure and laziness.

Sea Urchins

~

This time we are going to start our meal with a platter of sea urchins, and I have some advice on how to fish for them. Even if you can find beautiful sea urchins at a good fishmonger, the pleasure of eating them is far greater when you have caught them yourself and can savour them on the spot.

Like oysters and mussels, you do not fish for sea urchins from May to September, the period of reproduction. But we are in April, the weather is glorious and the sea is calm; never mind if the urchins are not quite as perfect as in February. Plastic sandals are necessary because sea urchin spines are painful. Take along a canvas potato sack to store your catch and a bucket with a glass bottom, which we call *une glace* (a mirror) around here, so as to be able to see the sea bed clearly. You can also arm yourself with an old fork which will be helpful to scrape the urchins off the rocks if you are worried about your fingers. Personally, I prefer to use my hands, and with a little practice it is perfectly safe. On the rocks, you will see urchins of all kinds and colours. All the small ones, purple, blue, red or green, are good, but do not take the big black ones. They will be empty and will be a waste of time and effort. When you bring them back to the *cabanon*, leave them in the wet canvas bag until lunchtime, taking care to keep the bag moist.

Open the sea urchins at the very last minute, and to do that you will need to sacrifice a pair of old kitchen scissors which you will not be able to use for anything else afterwards! Cut an opening at the base of the shell, around the mouth. Be careful not to damage the coral inside. Once you have done 2 or 3 urchins, you will have got the knack. You can pour out the sea water and scrape off the brown bits to leave only the red coral, but true sea urchin *aficionados* eat everything.

Eat your sea urchins as soon as they are ready, with little fingers of bread, the way you would eat a soft-boiled egg. Do not add lemon juice or vinegar: the flavour of the urchins is perfect on its own.

Chips,
Vinsobres Style

~

WINE:
Vinsobres
rouge

People who have never tasted my friend Hélène's chips cannot understand how on earth large potato sticks cooked in a frying pan of olive oil can taste so good. The secret is simple and Hélène agreed to share it with me. Wash and peel 6–7 large potatoes and cut them into thick chips. Heat 1 cm (½ inch) of olive oil in a large frying pan over a medium heat. Dry the chips thoroughly before adding them to the oil, which should be hot, but not smoking. Cooking must be slow, the oil bubbling around the potatoes, which will gradually acquire a nice golden colour. If the oil is too hot, they will darken too quickly without being cooked. If the oil is not hot enough, the chips will absorb too much fat and will remain pale and limp. Turn them carefully with a fork to allow them to brown evenly on all sides.

The real secret comes after about 10 minutes: throw into the pan at least a dozen unpeeled garlic cloves and let them cook alongside the chips, constantly turning them over. This causes a strange alchemy which imparts to the chips not only flavour but also a particular texture which is like no other. When the chips are nicely crusty and golden, transfer them to a serving dish lined with kitchen paper. Season generously with sea salt, tossing the potatoes in the dish to distribute the salt evenly. Serve them immediately.

Personally, I do not know of any chips that taste better than these. As a matter of fact, they are a dish on their own, ideal as a first course or with a green salad, even though they make a perfect accompaniment to grilled fish or meat.

Sea urchin

The Baron's
Sea Bream

~

Our baron is from Toulon and he is a fisherman. In fact, I should call him a gardener of the sea, because he goes to sea the way you or I have a walk around the garden, and he always brings back fish for the meal, fish so fresh that it still wriggles in his basket. The recipe is rustic and easy, so its success will depend upon the freshness and quality of the fish. The royal sea bream is of course a fish fit for kings, but other members of the bream family will do just as well for this recipe.

IN THE KITCHEN : Prepare a good fire with vine stumps or cuttings.
Scale a sea bream and clean it out well, but do not wash it. Dry it carefully.
Season the inside of the fish with sea salt and freshly ground pepper, and stuff with slices of fennel and a handful of sage leaves. Let it stand for a while.
In a bowl, make a vinaigrette with sea salt, freshly ground pepper, olive oil and a little vinegar.
Make a little brush by tying a bunch of fresh sage leaves to a wooden stick about 30 cm (12 inches) long. This brush will be used to baste the bream with the vinaigrette while it is cooking. You will have to baste it often so it does not dry out. That is the secret of this recipe.
Place the fish in a hinged grill and let it cook over the hot coals for about 10 minutes on each side. To check if the fish is cooked, test with the tip of a knife between the gill and the backbone. The cooking time will depend, of course, on the size of the fish.
When the fish is ready, throw the brush into the fire, because you will not be able to use it again.

The bream can also be baked in the oven and will still be delicious.
Serve it with fennel and tomatoes (see recipe on page 158).

WINE :
Coteaux d'Aix en Provence blanc

A sage brush

Fennel and Tomatoes
~

This is the perfect accompaniment for our bream. In a heavy-bottomed pan, heat a little olive oil and gently cook 2 roughly chopped onions and a handful of diced bacon, until the onion is soft. Add 6 large fennel bulbs, cut in half, 5–6 unpeeled garlic cloves, a glass of dry white wine, some sea salt and freshly ground pepper. Simmer for 10 minutes, then add 6 ripe tomatoes, halved or a jar of preserved tomatoes (see recipe on page 159). Cover and simmer for about 1 hour.

Salt Cod, Grandet Style
~

WINE:
Coteaux d'Aix
en Provence
rosé

Here is a recipe for lazy cooks because, at the *cabanon*, one feels more like lazing around than cooking all day. Choose some nice salted but not dried cod fillets. Rinse the fish carefully under running water and soak it for a couple of hours only. You do not need to soak it for 24 hours because you are going to poach it in a large quantity of water and you want it to impart its flavour and saltiness to the vegetables.

To a large cooking pot full of boiling water, add some carrots, some leeks, old potatoes, turnips, pieces of pumpkin and fennel, all of which should have been washed, peeled and chopped into large pieces. Add a splash of olive oil, 2 bay leaves, a few peppercorns, but no salt. Cook the vegetables for 30 minutes and, when they are tender, add the drained cod. Turn off the heat and let the fish poach in the vegetable broth for about 10 minutes. Drain and serve, drizzled with a little olive oil. The cod will still be a little salty but eaten with the vegetables, it will be delicious.

Tomato Preserve
and Tomato Coulis
~

It is a fact that you can now buy excellent canned tomatoes in the shops. But if you happen to be on holiday in July, when tomatoes are cheap, and you feel like savouring the pleasures of a bygone era, make some tomato preserve following these recipes. Then you can store them at the *cabanon*.

First, we will make jars of whole tomatoes. You will need firm tomatoes, not too ripe. Wash and dry them. Cut them in half and take out the seeds. Then pack the tomatoes into some sterilized glass jars and top up the jars with lightly salted water. Seal the jars and then place them in a sterilizer or large laundry boiler with some straw or hay around them to prevent breakages. Fill the boiler with cold water. Place it over the heat and bring the water to the boil. Sterilize the jars for 15 minutes, at a rolling boil.

For the *coulis*, we are going to preserve a purée of tomatoes without any seasoning. Of course, this *coulis* is not meant to be used as is. Use it in winter, when fresh tomatoes are rare, expensive and tasteless, as a base for delicious sauces (see recipe on page 140).

You need large ripe tomatoes. Peel and seed them (to peel them more easily, plunge them into boiling water for 2 minutes). I should add that tomato skin gives sauces a delicious flavour, but is totally indigestible. Chop the tomato flesh and cook it for 15 minutes. Then press through a sieve and pour it straight into some sterilized jars (in the old days, they used to keep the *coulis* in champagne bottles). Seal the jars and sterilize them (the method is the same as for whole tomatoes) for an hour. Let them cool before taking them out of the sterilizer.

Spaghetti
'au Monstre'

~

First, we are going to braise *le monstre*. *Le monstre* is a 1–1.5 kg (2–3 lb) octopus. Any larger, and the flesh will be too rubbery. It should not be too fresh either, because then the skin would be too tough. Ideally the octopus should be caught at least the day before and kept for up to 36 hours in the refrigerator.

First, it has to be beaten against a rock, rather hard and for quite a while (do not worry, it is dead by now) to soften the flesh. Then remove the hard beak and the innards, but not the skin.

In a large flameproof pot, lightly brown 4 peeled garlic cloves in some olive oil. Discard this garlic and add 1.5 kg (3 lb) of ripe tomatoes, peeled and chopped (or use a jar of preserved tomatoes). Add a small hot chilli and some freshly ground pepper.

Salt will be added at the end because the octopus might release some sea water while it is cooking. Cook the sauce for 20 minutes, then add the octopus. Simmer, covered, for 1–1½ hours, depending on the size of your octopus.

Check if the octopus is cooked by pricking it with a fork, which should penetrate easily. If the sauce is too runny, reduce it by boiling it, uncovered, for a little while, first removing the octopus and keeping it warm. Taste the sauce and add salt if necessary, as well as a large handful of chopped parsley.

Cook the spaghetti in a large pan of boiling salted water until *al dente*. Drain the pasta and, just before serving, toss everything together in a large bowl: the spaghetti, the sauce and *le monstre*.

Wine:
Coteaux d'Aix
en Provence,
Les Baux rouge

*Spaghetti 'au
Monstre'*

Spaghetti
with Clams
~

WINE:
Palette
blanc

Pour a little olive oil into a deep, wide pan over a low heat, then slowly cook 2 chopped garlic cloves and 1 small chopped hot chilli, until the garlic is golden brown. Add 1 kg (2 lb) of washed clams, cover the pan and cook over a low heat for a few minutes until the shells have opened. Discard any that remain closed. Toss the clams with 500 g (1 lb) of spaghetti (cooked *al dente*) and a good handful of chopped parsley. Serve straight away with some grated cheese.

Auntie Anne's
Spaghetti with Sausage
~

WINE:
Palette
rosé

In a cast-iron pan, brown 3 garlic cloves in some peanut oil, then remove the garlic cloves and keep on one side. In the same oil, brown a few garlic sausages, a few pork chops and some pieces of streaky bacon. When they are nice and golden, take them out and keep warm. To the pan, add 1 kg (2 lb) of ripe tomatoes, peeled and chopped, or a jar of tomato preserve. Add the garlic cloves, a few basil leaves, some sea salt and freshly ground pepper and 1 lump of sugar. Let the sauce simmer gently for 30 minutes, then put all the meats back in the pan and cook for another 15 minutes or so.
Serve with spaghetti (cooked *al dente*) and some grated cheese.

Navettes
~

Navettes (shuttles) are pale blond biscuits, flavoured with orange-flower water, in the shape of the little shuttles used by weavers in the old days. When I was a child in Aix, we used to buy them from the biscuit factory on *rue des Tanneurs* (Weaver Street). When the oven was hot, we could smell the biscuits cooking from the bottom of *rue des Cordeliers* to the top of *rue Espariat*. Of course, the biscuit factory on Weaver Street has long gone, but here is a rather good recipe for *navettes*.

In the kitchen : Make a syrup by boiling 100 ml (3½ fl oz) of water with 125 g (4 oz) of sugar for 5 minutes. Allow the syrup to cool. In a bowl, sift 300 g (10 oz) of flour with a pinch of salt, add 150 g (5 oz) of softened butter and rub in until the mixture resembles fine bread-crumbs. Pour the syrup on to this mixture with 1 tablespoon of orange-flower water. Mix well to get a smooth and supple dough. Roll out the dough to a thickness of 8 mm (⅓ inch), then use a knife to cut out lozenges 7 cm (3 inches) long. Make a deep slit along the length of the biscuits, without cutting right to the ends. Butter a baking sheet and place the *navettes* on it. Bake for about 20 minutes in a moderate oven. They should not brown. Let them cool completely before packing them into a tin and taking them to the *cabanon*.

Navettes

Brousse Cheese from Rove

~

Brousse cheese is a delicious fresh goats' cheese which has been made in Rove for as long as I can remember, on Rove Hill, close to Marseilles, between Estaque and Redonne. It is prepared in rather unusual small containers, long and narrow, which are pierced at the bottom to allow the cheeses to drain. The containers used to be made of blown glass or woven straw. Today, they are made of plastic, but this has not made any difference to the quality of the cheese.

Young goatherds used to come and sell their produce in the streets of Marseilles, and even as far as Aix. Carrying their produce in large wicker baskets which hung from their necks and blowing a little trumpet they would shout, 'Brousse cheese from the Rove'. I can still remember hearing them. Today there are no more street sellers in Aix, but thankfully there are still a few goats on the Rove and you can still find the cheese at good dairies and markets. Brousse cheese is best eaten fresh with a dash of rum and some caster sugar, or with a good jam like this fig jam.

Fig Jam

~

You should make this jam in September, when figs are sweet and plump. Actually we should call this preserve candied figs, because we are going to leave them whole. Choose figs that are firm and not too ripe. Prick each fig several times with a needle. Blanch the figs in boiling water, drain them well and place them in a preserving pan with 750 g (1½ lb) of sugar per 1 kg (2 lb) of fruit. Leave them to stand until the following day. Cook the figs until the syrup thickens enough to cover a wooden spoon without dripping. Add a good-sized glass of rum, boil for a further couple of minutes, then pour into sterilized jars.

The 'cabanon'

LUNCH ON THE
TERRACE

People here have never understood why in the middle of August, most tourists insist on having lunch in the hot midday sun. It seems pure folly to see all these pale bodies determined on burning and turning lobster-red. In a country that has invented the afternoon siesta, not because of a natural inclination to laziness, but because you have worked in the fields half the night, it is natural and refreshing to rest during the hottest part of the day. The people of Provence love the sun in winter and the shade in summer. That is why they grow trees like elm and mulberry in front of their houses to provide the necessary shade. But, later in the year, when the time has come, the trees will shed their leaves to let the light and the warmth through. This is also why often they grow a vine on the side of their houses. They can then set a table under its shade during the warm season. Lunch on the vine-covered terrace starts rather early, around 11:30, with a drink. Feeling relaxed after enjoying a glass of homemade walnut or orange wine, your taste-buds will have been nicely titillated by crusty golden fritters of courgette blossoms and the marvellous smell coming from the *soupe au pistou* in the kitchen. This, according to *les Provençaux*, is the best way to work up a good appetite . . .

Orange wine served on a covered terrace

Red and white beans for soupe au pistou

167

Olga's Walnut Wine

~

In June, cut 25 whole green walnuts (shells included) into quarters. Let them macerate in 1 litre (1¾ pints) of eau-de-vie with a split vanilla pod. After a month, filter the alcohol and pour it into a demi-john with 5 litres (8 pints) of good red wine and 1 kg (2 lb) of sugar. Let the mixture age in a dark, cool place for at least 5 months, then decant into sterilized bottles. Seal the bottles securely and wait another 6 months before tasting your walnut wine.

Orange Wine

~

You should make this wine in January. Take a large glass container with a lid. Fill it with 2 lemons, 5 sweet oranges and 5 bitter oranges, all washed, dried and quartered. Add 5 litres (8 pints) of good white wine and 1 litre (1¾ pints) of eau-de-vie. Add 1 kg (2 lb) of caster sugar and a split vanilla pod. Seal the container and store it in a dark, cool place. After 2 months, you can decant the wine into bottles, which need to be sealed carefully. Like the walnut wine, you will have to wait at least 6 months before drinking it. Serve it chilled or with ice cubes.

Courgette and Courgette Blossom Fritters

~

With your aperitif you can treat your guests to these delicious courgette fritters and courgette blossom fritters. Choose smallish very fresh courgettes with smooth, tender skin so you will not have to peel them. The blossoms must be firm and open.

First, make a spicy tomato *coulis*: heat a

little olive oil and brown a crushed clove of garlic and 1–2 hot chillies for a couple of seconds. Then add chopped tomatoes, a little salt, a sugar lump and a few basil leaves. Cover and simmer for 1 hour. When the *coulis* is ready, let it cool. You should serve it cool, but not chilled.

Now make a fairly liquid batter by mixing some flour and water with a whisk. Season with sea salt and freshly ground pepper.

Then prepare the vegetables. Remove the pistil and the stem from the blossoms and cut the courgettes into thin slices. You could also add 2 potatoes, peeled and finely sliced, if wished.

Make the fritters at the last moment, they must be served piping hot.

In a large frying pan, heat at least 2.5 cm (1 inch) of peanut oil. With a fork, dip the courgette and potato slices, if using, and the blossoms, into the batter, then straight into the hot oil.

Brown the fritters on both sides and let them drain on absorbent paper on a warm plate. Serve them straight away with the tomato *coulis*.

A Jar of Anchovies
~

Spring is the best time to prepare these. At the fishmongers, choose nice plump anchovies, absolutely fresh. The success of this recipe depends upon this. Do not wash them but wipe them carefully. Do not gut them either. In a large *tian*, let the anchovies marinate for 3 hours in their own weight of table salt. They should be completely buried in the salt. Do not use coarse salt because then you would have to salt them a lot longer. After 3 hours, remove the anchovies from the salt, and soak them in white vinegar for another 3 hours. After that, you can fillet the anchovies and arrange them in a sterilized preserving jar with some chopped garlic and parsley and cover them with some good olive oil. Keep the jar in a cool place, and use the anchovies within 1 month. But do not forget to bring the jar to room temperature a few hours before serving. Eat these anchovies with bread and butter. That way, they are absolutely delicious.

Pages 170–171:
Bruno Carles' 'mas de Malherbes' in Camargue

Auntie Lilette's
Soupe au Pistou

~

Place 250 g (8 oz) of white haricot beans, 250 g (8 oz) of red haricot beans, 400 g (13 oz) of large green beans cut in half, 2 courgettes, 3 potatoes, cut into large cubes, and 2 white onions, roughly chopped, in about 3 litres (5 pints) of salted water. That is all. Do not be tempted to add a few carrots for colour because their taste would alter the flavour of the basil. Cook these vegetables gently for about 2 hours. After 1½ hours, remove all the pieces of potato and courgette, and mash them together, before returning them to the pot.

Now we are going to make the *pistou*. Cook 3 whole tomatoes in the soup for 30 minutes. Then, take them out using a slotted spoon, peel the tomatoes and let them cool in a colander. In a large marble mortar, mash 1 generous handful of basil leaves with 7 garlic cloves. The pungent aroma produced is mouthwatering. Then add the peeled tomatoes and 5 tablespoons of fruity extra-virgin olive oil. Keep mashing. Finally, add 150 g (5 oz) of grated cheese. The best cheese for this soup is *le rouge* (red cheese – Dutch Edam coloured with annatto) from Holland, but alternatively you can use Gruyère or

Parmesan cheese. Pepper generously and mix well with your wooden pestle until you have a smooth paste.

A few minutes before serving, add 3 handfuls of *lumache* (elbow) pasta to the soup. When the pasta is cooked, take the soup off the heat and let it cool a little before adding the *pistou*. Serve immediately or serve it cold the following day.

This thick soup is, of course, very nourishing and since it is so delicious, one has a tendency to have a second helping. In which case it should be the main course of your meal with just a green salad, then a tray of goats' cheese and a good dessert to follow.

Radish Leaf
or Nettle Soup
~

Here is a lighter and more economical soup, which will make a delicious first course and amuse your friends. It is a spring soup, which should be made when radishes are tender, and nettle shoots, bright and green, have just appeared in the fields.

Either take the greens from a large bunch of fresh young radishes or go and pick a bunch of nettle shoots. If you do not touch the top of the leaves, you will not be stung; alternatively you can wear gloves. Wash the leaves and throw away the stalks. In a large pan, melt a large knob of butter, add the leaves, and cook until soft. Add 4 potatoes, washed, peeled and finely sliced. Cover with water and season with sea salt, freshly ground pepper and freshly grated nutmeg. Simmer gently for 30 minutes. Meanwhile, in a bowl, mix 3 tablespoons of fresh single cream with an egg yolk. Take the pan off the heat and add a little soup to the cream and egg mixture. Then pour this mixture into the soup, stir thoroughly, warm through being careful not to let the soup boil, and serve straight away.

My Mother's
Salt Cod Gratin
~

Soak the salt cod for 24 hours, changing the water frequently. Poach it for 15 minutes in simmering water, but do not let it boil. Drain the cod, remove and discard the skin and bones, and flake the fish. In a flameproof gratin dish, heat a little olive oil and brown 2 onions, the white of 2 leeks and 2 garlic cloves, all finely chopped. When they are golden, add the fish, then cover the fish with a layer of sliced potatoes which have been parboiled. Finish with a layer of ripe tomatoes, sliced fairly thickly.

Bake in a moderate oven for 15 minutes. Then add a dash of olive oil and some grated cheese. Return to the oven for a further 20 minutes or so until the gratin is golden. Take it out of the oven and let it set and cool for a few minutes before serving.

Wine:
Côtes
du Rhône
rosé

Tian of
Glazed Aubergines

~

You will need 4 or 5 medium-sized aubergines, shiny and firm. Pick the same quantity of both tomatoes and white onions, which have a similar diameter to the aubergines. Wash and dry the aubergines and the tomatoes, but do not peel them. Peel the onions though. Cut all the vegetables into 5 mm (¼ inch) thick slices. Now you are going to arrange alternate slices in an earthenware gratin dish – aubergine, onion, tomato, aubergine, onion, tomato and so on. Do not layer them horizontally, but place them skin-side up, see picture on the facing page. The vegetables must be packed tightly together, leaving no room in the dish. Fill in any cracks with peeled garlic cloves. Sprinkle with sea salt, freshly ground pepper, some fresh thyme and marjoram and a generous helping of olive oil.

Bake in a moderate oven for about 20 minutes. Then take the dish out of the oven and gently press on the vegetables with a slotted spoon, to allow the juices to mingle. Be careful not to crush the vegetables. Return to the oven for a further 40 minutes. If you wish, 15 minutes before serving, you can sprinkle some grated cheese over the top. The addition of cheese is delicious, but not essential.

Madame Cheynet's
Aubergines

~

Madame Cheynet was a friend of my mother's, who had adopted Provence as her home. She was a marvellous cook and to our great delight adapted an old recipe for potatoes with bacon, by substituting the potatoes with aubergines. Here is Madame Cheynet's recipe:

Choose small aubergines, plump and squat. Wash and dry, but do not peel them. Split the aubergines lengthways on one side, but do not cut right through, so that the 2 halves will not be completely separated. Inside the aubergines, place a thin slice of streaky bacon and tie the aubergines up with some string. Into a cast-iron pot, pour a little peanut oil. Add the aubergines with a large onion, chopped, and 3–4 ripe tomatoes that you

*A tian o
glaze
aubergine.
and 'le.
petits farcis*

will have quartered. Season with sea salt and freshly ground pepper. Be careful not to add too much salt because of the bacon. Cover and cook over a low heat for a good hour. To finish off the dish, remove the lid and continue to cook the aubergines for a little longer, to allow any excess liquid to evaporate. These aubergines are delicious served warm, or even cold the following day.

Courgette Gratin
~

For 1 kg (2 lb) of courgettes you will need 400 g (13 oz) of white onions. Clean the courgettes. Do not peel, but slice them. Peel and chop the onions. Cook the vegetables in boiling salted water for 30 minutes. Drain well, then mash the vegetables in a gratin dish with a fork. Stir in a little butter, 1–2 tablespoons of flour to bind and 2 tablespoons of fresh single cream. Cook for 2–3 minutes. Sprinkle over some grated cheese, and lightly press it down with a fork, then add a handful of breadcrumbs and bake for 15 minutes in a moderate oven.

Unlike the *tian* of glazed aubergines, this gratin is not a dish in itself, but it is a perfect accompaniment for grilled meat or roast lamb.

'Les petits farcis'
~

For these stuffed vegetables, you will need 1 tomato, 1 aubergine, 1 pattypan squash and 1 green pepper per person. Choose pretty, plump and round vegetables that are not too large. Greengrocers nowadays sell different varieties of squash and aubergines which would be perfect for this recipe.

Wash and dry the vegetables. Slice off the top of the tomatoes, and with a spoon remove any seeds and excess water. Cut off the top of the peppers and remove the seeds and membranes from the inside. Tail the aubergines with a sharp knife, then with a teaspoon, hollow the centre. Make sure you do not damage the skin, and keep the flesh you are removing. Do the same with the round pattypan squash.

Now we are going to prepare the stuffings, which will be different for each vegetable. Chop each of the stuffing ingredients separately, then you will mix them together with some grated cheese, some rice (which will absorb any vegetable juice) and 2 whole eggs to bind everything together.

For the tomatoes: mince some leftover beef from a *daube* or boiled beef. Then chop 2 garlic cloves, 1 onion, 1 tomato, peeled and seeded, and the flesh of the pattypan squash. In a frying pan, brown the onion in a little olive oil, then add the garlic, the other vegetables, and finally the meat. Take the pan off the heat, and add 1 cupful of Camargue round rice (short-grain rice), 2 whole eggs, a handful of grated cheese, a pinch of sugar, sea salt and some freshly ground pepper.

For the aubergines: mince some leftover lamb, from a roast for instance. Then chop 2 garlic cloves, 1 onion, the flesh of 2 tomatoes and the flesh of the aubergines. Heat a little olive oil and brown the onion, then the aubergine flesh, followed by the garlic and tomato. Add a handful of Camargue round rice, a handful of grated cheese, a handful of pine nuts, 2 whole eggs, some sea salt and freshly ground pepper.

For the green peppers: mince some cooked ham and chop the flesh of 1 red pepper and 1 tomato, 2 garlic cloves and 1 onion. Brown the onion in a little olive oil, then add the pepper, the garlic and finally the tomato. Add the ham with a handful of Camargue round rice, a handful of grated cheese, 2 whole eggs, and some sea salt and freshly ground pepper.

Finally, for the squash: brown 1 chopped onion in a little olive oil, add 150 g (5 oz) of fresh Brousse goats' cheese, a handful of Camargue round rice, a handful of grated cheese, 2 whole eggs and some freshly chopped parsley. Season with a little sea salt and some freshly ground pepper.

Fill the vegetables with their respective stuffings. Arrange them side by side in a large gratin dish. Sprinkle with breadcrumbs and drizzle with a little olive oil. Bake in a warm oven for at least 2 hours. The vegetables must be glazed and golden at the end of this cooking time. Allow *les petits farcis* to cool for at least 10 minutes before serving.

WINE:
Côtes
du Rhône
rosé

Lambs' Trotters and
Tripe Bundles 'à la Marseillaise'

~

At the tripe shop or the butchers, choose 2 lambs' stomachs (tripe) and 8 lambs' trotters as well as a generous 750 g (1½ lb) of calf's caul (the membrane which encloses the stomach). Wash these carefully under cold running water. Cut the tripe into rectangular pieces approximately 10 x 5 cm (4 x 2 inches). Roll the tripe around pieces of streaky bacon and tie these little bundles with stretched strips of the calf's caul. A lot of people chop up the streaky bacon with garlic and parsley, but my Grandmother Athalie Pascal never did. Neither do I, as I do not like it like that.

WINE:
Côtes
du Rhône
rosé

In a deep earthenware dish, with a lid, arrange the lambs' trotters and the bundles on a mixture of sliced carrots, bacon bits, thinly sliced onions, the flesh of a few tomatoes, peeled and chopped, a sliced celery stick, and 1–2 finely chopped garlic cloves. Season with sea salt and freshly ground pepper. You can add 2–3 cloves if you are partial to their flavour. You need to mix the meat with the vegetables and moisten the mixture with a glass of white wine. Make a ribbon of dough with a little flour and water and

use it to seal the lid onto the earthenware dish (as long as the lid has a small hole to allow the steam to escape). Place the covered dish in a slow oven and bake for 6–7 hours.

This is a spring or summer time recipe, using fresh tomatoes. Here is a winter recipe for lambs' trotters and bundles which is also very tasty.

Delicious Trotters and Tripe Bundles

~

Prepare the lambs' tripe as in the previous recipe. We are now simply going to stuff the bundles with a different mixture, by chopping together 100 g (3½ oz) of streaky bacon and 100 g (3½ oz) of fresh truffles, and finally adding 50 g (2 oz) of cured raw ham, finely diced.

Heat a little olive oil in a glazed earthenware pot, and slowly brown 1 onion, 1 carrot and 1 stick of celery, all finely chopped. Arrange the trotters on these vegetables, then add the tripe bundles. Add 1 cup of tomato *coulis* (see recipe on page 159), 2 garlic cloves, 2 cloves (optional), a little thyme and 2 bay leaves. Moisten with 1 glass of white wine and 2 glasses of broth. Season lightly with sea salt and freshly ground pepper. Cover the pot, sealing the lid on with a ribbon of dough (as long as the lid has a small hole to allow the steam to escape), and bake in a slow oven for 6–7 hours.

WINE: Hermitage rouge

Tomatoes 'à la provençale'

~

For this very simple and delicious dish you must choose unblemished round tomatoes, bright red, but still firm. Wash and dry the tomatoes, and then cut them into halves. Carefully remove and discard the seeds and any excess water. Cook the tomato halves, cut side down, in a frying pan with a little olive oil over a high heat. After a few minutes, turn the tomatoes over and cook the other side. Lower the heat, and let them simmer for at least 10 minutes. Then transfer the tomato halves to an oiled baking dish or *tian*. They should be packed fairly tightly together. Sprinkle with sea salt, freshly ground pepper, and a pinch of sugar to counteract the acidity of the tomatoes. Then add a generous amount of chopped garlic and parsley, and finally scatter a few breadcrumbs over the top.

Drizzle a little olive oil over the tomatoes, and bake them in a warm oven until the tomatoes are almost caramelized.

Fig Gratin

~

In the province of Comtat, towards the end of the summer, we make a truly beautiful dessert with figs. For this recipe small Caromb figs are ideal, but any other variety of autumn fig, fully ripe and plump, will do. The people of Provence have adapted the classic recipe of baked apples by using figs, and it tastes even better.

IN THE KITCHEN : Wash and dry the figs and tail, but do not peel them. Cut a cross on the top of each fig and lightly squeeze to allow them to open a little. Arrange them in tightly packed rows, cut side up, in a fairly high-sided gratin dish. Sprinkle with a good measure of fruit alcohol, pear or raspberry, and place a little knob of butter on each fig. Sprinkle with a little sugar (not too much, figs are naturally sweet) and bake in a slow oven for at least 1½ hours.
Serve warm, but not hot, with thick fresh double cream or chantilly cream (see the recipe on page 196).

Apricot Gratin

~

In a bowl, mix by hand 100 g (3½ oz) each of plain flour, ground almonds and sugar, and then add a pinch of salt. Rub in 150 g (5 oz) of softened butter until the mixture resembles fine breadcrumbs. Add to this crumble 100 g (3½ oz) of pine nuts and 100 g (3½ oz) of blanched almonds. In an earthenware gratin dish, arrange the large ripe apricots, halved and stoned, cut side up. Then simply cover the apricots with the crumble mixture and bake for 1 hour in a slow oven. Serve warm, like the Fig Gratin, this dessert is delicious accompanied by thick fresh double cream or chantilly cream (see the recipe on page 196).

ig gratin and
ricot gratin

A GARDEN FEAST

Today is a day of celebration in the big pink house. Yesterday, the aunties and children went to a small wood to gather branches of box (an evergreen shrub) for their dark-green table garlands. And this morning, as soon as the dew had evaporated, we draped the long tables with white linen cloths and hung the garlands in large festoons around them. Then, we brought out the glasses and carafes, and polished the silver. We built pyramids of red apples and muscat grapes, using toothpicks to hold the apples together. All over the house people were busy, arranging bouquets, breaking blocks of ice to chill the bottles of wine in the fountain, and all of this amidst laughter in the most organized havoc. The summer holidays are coming to an end, and we are going to hold a banquet in the garden as we do every year. The house is happy. Hordes of dogs and cousins are running everywhere. In the drawing room near the piano, like actors for a day, we are rehearsing the show that will be staged in the afternoon. In the linen room, final adjustments are being made to the costumes. In the kitchen, cooks are busy preparing the *aïoli*.

*Wine cooling
the
fountain*

'Le Grand Aïoli'

~

Aïoli can be a sauce or it can be the whole meal! The sauce with garlic and olive oil, strong and flavourful, is wonderful and a real taste of Provence. The meal can be a simple boiled dish, without meat, the kind of meal we would eat normally

WINE:
Côtes
du Luberon
rosé

on a Friday. But, with the *aïoli* this will be transformed into a magnificent feast.

IN THE KITCHEN : First you need a few large thick fillets of salted cod that have been soaked in water for 24 hours, with at least 4 changes of water. When the salt has been removed, poach the fish for about 20 minutes without allowing

it to boil. The water must barely simmer. You can serve the cod warm or cold.

Then prepare the vegetables: potatoes cooked in their skins and served hot; whole carrots, peeled and boiled; 1–2 small cauliflowers, nice and white, steamed until *al dente*; courgettes boiled in their skins; beetroot, boiled then peeled; leeks, lightly boiled; green beans, blanched, and finally artichokes, steamed. Each vegetable must be cooked separately. You will also need hard-boiled eggs, shelled, of course. Finally you need a few little grey snails that you will have fed with flour, to cleanse them, for 3 weeks prior to your feast. On the day the snails should be poached for 20 minutes in salted water with a few herbs (some sprigs of thyme and 2 bay leaves).

Then prepare the sauce in a large marble mortar using a wooden pestle. Mash a dozen garlic cloves until you have a smooth paste. Add 2 egg yolks, which have been kept at room temperature. Work the *aïoli* like a mayonnaise, using a whisk instead of the pestle. Pour in the olive oil, which also should be at room temperature, little by little, to begin with, and a little faster later, whisking all the time until the *aïoli* is thick and smooth. Add a touch of salt. That is all.

This is a very strongly flavoured dish which is best accompanied by red wine. It is, by definition, a summer feast, and would be sufficient on its own, but some finnicky eaters might balk at the idea. So, to please them as well, we have prepared a selection of other dishes, lighter and more conventional, but equally as delicious.

Little Green Pies

~

It is necessary to start this dish by going for a walk. The wild herbs, that you will collect on your country stroll, will give your pies their distinctive green colour. You can, of course, use only spinach or the green part of Swiss chard that you can buy at the market, but it will taste far better if you add some wild herbs such as rocket, young nettle shoots, and tender dandelion leaves gathered along country lanes, and wild leeks growing in the vineyards. Back in the kitchen, you

need to sort and wash the herbs and spinach. Drain them well and chop coarsely. The ideal proportion is half spinach, half wild herbs. You can add a lettuce heart, which would give a delicate, slightly bitter flavour, and some herbs from the garden, but sparingly.

Pour a little olive oil into a large frying pan, warm over a low heat and then add the herb mixture. Allow the herbs to wilt slowly until all their water has evaporated and they are starting to dry out. Add some sea salt and lots of freshly ground black pepper. Let the herbs and spinach cool.

Meanwhile, make some puff pastry with 500 g (1 lb) of flour and 250 g (8 oz) of butter, a pinch of salt and a little cold water. This will give you a fairly light puff pastry; if you would like it richer, add more butter. Give it 4 turns, and roll it out to a 1 cm (½ inch) thick sheet. Then, cut out rectangles, about 10 x 6 cm (4 x 2½ inches). On half of the rectangles, place 1 tablespoon of the herb and spinach mixture and then cover them with the other pastry rectangles, making sure you seal the edges completely, using a little water. With the tip of a knife, make a few decorative slits in the pie crust. Brush with a little beaten egg and cook in a fairly hot oven until the pies are puffed and golden. As with all puff pastry, these pies are best served warm.

Aubergines 'à la provençale' or 'à la bohémienne'

~

In both cases the dish consists of a plate of fried aubergines, served cold, with a good flavourful tomato *coulis*.

When you prepare the aubergines by cutting them lengthways, the dish is called aubergines '*à la provençale*'. When the aubergines are cut into small dice, it is called '*à la bohémienne*'.

In the kitchen : First, we are going to prepare the fresh tomato *coulis*. Choose some perfectly ripened tomatoes. Wash and quarter them. Into a pan pour a little olive oil, heat it gently and add the tomatoes, some sea salt, sugar, 2 garlic cloves and a bouquet garni. Allow the sauce to simmer over a low heat for at least 30 minutes. The sauce is ready when it is nice and thick. Let it cool. If you prefer a smooth sauce, then strain the *coulis* through a sieve at this point.

Now for the aubergines: wash and dry, but do not peel them. Either slice them lengthways, or dice them into 1 cm (½ inch) cubes, depending on whether you are preparing aubergines '*à la bohémienne*' or '*à la provençale*'. If you have time, sprinkle the aubergines with coarse sea salt and leave for 2–3 hours, to allow them to release any excess water. This will mean the aubergines will absorb less oil when you fry them. If you salt them, you will have to squeeze the water out by hand. Do not worry about them being too salty.

Fry the aubergines in hot olive oil. As soon as they are golden on all sides remove and allow them to drain on absorbent kitchen paper. When they are thoroughly drained, arrange the slices of aubergine on a platter around the tomato *coulis* and you have aubergines '*à la provençale*'. Or mix the diced aubergines with just enough *coulis* to coat them and they are '*à la bohémienne*'.

*Orange Tabbouleh and Aubergine '*à la bohémienne*'*

Ratatouille

~

Like the aubergines '*à la provençale*' and '*à la bohémienne*', ratatouille can be served cold as a first course. Served hot, it is delicious with grilled lamb or rabbit cooked in mustard.

First, we are going to prepare the vegetables. Choose 4 large, shiny firm aubergines, 4 unblemished courgettes, 2 large red peppers, 5 very ripe tomatoes and 5 firm white onions. Wash and dry the aubergines and the courgettes. Tail, but do not peel them. Dice the flesh into 1 cm (½ inch) cubes. Wash and dry the red peppers, cut in half, remove the stalks, de-seed, core, and cut into pieces. Peel the ripe tomatoes, remove and discard the seeds and any excess water and dice the flesh. Peel the white onions, and chop them up roughly. You will also need a dozen unpeeled garlic cloves.

In a cast-iron pot, heat a little olive oil. First brown the onions, then add the red peppers and the aubergines and let them brown until they are a nice golden colour. Add the courgettes and allow to brown a little before adding the tomatoes, the garlic, 1 bay leaf, a sprig of thyme, some sea salt, freshly ground pepper and 1 teaspoon of sugar. Stir thoroughly, and increase the heat until the vegetables reach simmering point. Reduce the temperature, cover and cook gently for a further hour. After that time, remove the lid and continue cooking uncovered for a further hour or until all the excess liquid has evaporated. Stir occasionally whilst reducing the ratatouille to ensure the vegetables do not stick to the pan. Just before serving, add a finely chopped garlic clove to the vegetables. Grandmother Athalie Pascal used to call this 'throwing in a touch of garlic'. Stir the ratatouille and serve piping hot.

Omelette Gâteau

~

WINE:
Côtes
du Luberon
rosé

This omelette gâteau is served cold and sliced to show off its pretty colours. If you are feeding many guests, I suggest you make several small gâteaux instead of one large one.

Generously butter 1 large or several small round-bottomed Pyrex dishes. In each you will stack 5 omelettes of different flavours that will have been cooked one by one in a small frying pan, with the same diameter as the chosen dish.

Start with a spring onion omelette: in a pan brown the chopped spring onions in a little olive oil until they are soft. Take them out of the oil with a slotted spoon, and place them in a large bowl with 6 eggs. Lightly beat the eggs with a fork and season with a pinch of sea salt and freshly ground pepper. Heat the frying pan and add a little more olive oil, if necessary. Pour in the egg mixture and stir gently with a wooden spoon. The omelette must be cooked over a low heat, because it must stay moist and should not change colour. Do not flip the omelette over, place it cooked-side down in the Pyrex dish.

Omelette gâ

Pages 190-
Garden feast at
Châtea
l'Ange in Lum

Now for the spinach omelette: you will need a large handful of spinach leaves, washed, chopped and cooked until wilted in a frying pan with a little olive oil, sea salt and freshly ground pepper. Proceed as for the spring onion omelette and when cooked, stack it in the Pyrex dish.

The third omelette will be flavoured with garlic: 1 garlic clove, finely chopped, is added to the eggs before beating.

The fourth omelette is a tomato omelette: 2 large spoonfuls of tomato *coulis* flavoured with onion, garlic and thyme are added to the eggs before beating.

In the last omelette, you will add some finely chopped parsley and chives.

Bake the omelette gâteau in a bain-marie in the oven for about 20 minutes. Turn it out onto a serving dish and let it cool.

This dish can be prepared the day before.

Bernard's
Orange Tabbouleh
~

My friend Bernard is originally from Algiers, but Africa, the Orient and Provence have long had very close ties. Everyone was used to seeing characters looking like the Wise Men from the Bible get off the boat at Marseilles harbour. The people of Provence were not fazed by their caftans, turbans and spices. We were often the first in France to discover the strange and marvellous flavours brought in by the merchant ships which traded with Africa and the Middle East. Even today, in the rich markets of Provence, you will find turmeric and ginger, coriander, cinnamon, dried fruit and pickled lemons from Morocco, their scents mingling naturally with those of our native basil and marjoram.

My friend Bernard is also a marvellous cook, when he sets his mind to it. He can, like no other, play around with the tastes and flavours of this mythical place he originally came from. He has created this delicious, refreshing tabbouleh with orange, cool and delicate, perfect for a summer lunch.

IN THE KITCHEN : You will need to start the day before by peeling the rind of 4 large oranges and cutting it into very fine julienne strips.

Take a large earthenware dish and pour

into it 1 kg (2 lb) of medium-grained cous-cous. Moisten it with the juice of 10 oranges and 4 lemons. Add the orange rind and 200 g (7 oz) of golden sultanas. Mix well, cover the dish with aluminium foil and let it stand overnight.

The following day, crumble the couscous with your fingertips to remove the lumps. Then add 1 bunch of flat-leaf parsley and the same quantity of mint leaves, washed and finely chopped. Do not use a machine to chop the herbs or they will turn brown and slimy. Peel, seed and dice a few ripe, unblemished tomatoes and 2 large cucumbers. Add them to the couscous with some sea salt, plenty of freshly ground pepper and a few table-spoons of fruity, extra virgin olive oil.

Mix thoroughly, transfer to a serving dish and store covered in a cool place for at least 1–2 hours before serving.

Joséphine's Salad

~

Another exotic salad, named after the Empress who came from the islands. This is extremely simple and delicious: a handful of sultanas, soaked for a few hours in the juice of 2 lemons; a cold cooked chicken, skinned, boned and cut into pieces; a cold pork roast, cubed; a fresh coconut, cut into fine julienne strips; the flesh of a grapefruit, cubed; a pinch of curry powder, a pinch of salt and a gen-erous dash of olive oil.

Mix all these ingredients together, cover and store in a cool place for at least 2 hours before serving.

WINE: Condrieu

Curry and condrieu, a perfect marriage

Mimosa Pastaga's
Sunshine Chicken

~

Mimosa Pastaga radiates warmth like the sun itself. The happy light sparkling in her eyes, the gaiety of her laughter, the generosity of her cooking and the *joie de vivre* of her friends, always numerous at her table, are a delight to witness.

In the kitchen : The day before, prepare the marinade with 1 glass of olive oil, 1 tablespoon of sweet paprika, 1 tablespoon of turmeric, a pinch of sea salt and some freshly ground pepper.
Cut 2 large chickens into pieces and steep them in the marinade, then refrigerate overnight. The following day, in a pan, brown the chicken in the oil from the marinade until nice and golden. Then remove the chicken. In the same pan, brown 4 onions, coarsely chopped, 6 crushed garlic cloves, and 4 large ripe tomatoes, peeled, seeded and chopped. Add a piece of fresh root ginger, peeled and grated, and simmer for about 10 minutes. Return the chicken pieces to the pan and moisten with the juice of 2 lemons. Cook for a further 20 minutes over a low heat and add a few broken olives, both purple and green. Let the olives heat through, then arrange the chicken in a large serving dish and garnish with some quartered pickled lemons. You will find these pickled lemons with the olives at most markets in Provence.

Wine:
Condrieu

Milk Gratin

~

This is our version of egg custard: bring 1 litre (1¾ pints) of milk to the boil with 20 sugar lumps. Then allow the milk to cool slightly. In a bowl beat 6–7 eggs (depending on their size) with a fork and add 2 large tablespoons of rum. Mix the eggs into the warm milk, strain and then pour into a *tian*. Cook in a slow oven for 30 minutes or until the custard has set. You can also caramelize the bottom of the *tian*. Allow the caramel to harden before pouring in the egg and milk mixture. In that case, omit the rum. Serve warm or cold straight from the *tian*.

*Mimosa Pastaga's
Sunshine Chicken*

Chantilly Puffs

~

When I was a child, we would buy *petits choux* at the baker's every Sunday morning, and freshly made chantilly cream, at the dairy. The chantilly cream was whipped on demand, and only on Sunday mornings, in a huge noisy machine which worked with 2 large whisks. But what marvellous cream it was and what a difference compared to those horrible cans of ready-made chantilly people buy today!

If you are in Provence and if your local baker makes those little choux puffs called *bijoux de Nice*, and if your dairy whips up an authentic chantilly, then you do not need this recipe. But you will still enjoy filling the choux puffs with cream. This was my job and I am still licking my fingers. Just in case here goes . . .

IN THE KITCHEN : First we will make the choux pastry. In a saucepan, bring to the boil 500 ml (17 fl oz) of water, then add 200 g (7 oz) of butter, 15 g (½ oz) of salt and 25 g (1 oz) of sugar. When the mixture is boiling, add 400 g (13 oz) of flour all at once. Take the pan off the heat and beat vigorously with a wooden spoon until the dough stops sticking to the sides of the pan. Let the dough cool, then add 12 beaten eggs, one by one. Using an icing bag and nozzle, pipe your *petits choux* onto a buttered baking sheet and cook them for 30 minutes at 190°C (375°F) Gas Mark 5. Do remember to leave plenty of space between your *petits choux*, they will double in size when cooked.

As soon as you take them out of the oven, sprinkle them with sugar crystals (if you get on well with your baker, he will probably let you have some). Let the choux cool completely and just before serving, fill them with good chantilly by using a piping bag or by splitting them through the middle.

To make a successful chantilly cream you will need 250 ml (8 fl oz) of *crème fleurette* (single cream) and 250 ml (8 fl oz) of thick *crème double* (double cream). Keep them in the refrigerator for a few hours so they are well chilled. Of course, you will have chosen fresh, not sterilized cream. In a bowl, mix the creams, then whip them vigorously with a whisk until the chantilly is firm and frothy. Do not over-beat though, or it will turn to butter. Fold in 50 g (2 oz) of caster sugar with 2 teaspoons of vanilla sugar.

When win
colours sparkl
in the su

INDEX

~

acacia blossom fritters 108
'l'aïgo boulido' 61
aïoli, 'le grand' 184-5
almonds: almond and anchovy
        sauce 127
    almond and garlic sauce 126
    black nougat 68-9
    calissons 69
    crunchy almond biscuits 137
    my mother's almond log 75
anchovies: l'anchoïade 141
    anchovy quichets 126
    'brouffade' from the River Rhône
        84
    a jar of anchovies 169
apples: caramel and apple cake 52
    simple apple tart 51
apricot gratin 181
artichokes: artichoke omelette 100
    artichoke salad 71
    artichokes 'en barigoule' 104-6
    salad of purple artichokes 100
asparagus: truffles with Lauris 95
    wild asparagus omelette 95-6
aubergines: 'à la provençale' 186-7
    glazed aubergines tian 174
    grilled peppers and aubergines 119
    Jérôme's aubergine stew 117
    Madame Cheynet's aubergines
        174-6

beef: beef daube 148
    beef daube in jelly 145-6
    beef olives 85
    braised beef with carrots 81
    'brouffade' from the River Rhône
        84
biscuits: crunchy almond biscuits 137
    little vanilla crescents 56
    navettes 162-3
    rock biscuits 136
bouillabaisse 128-32
bread: olive bread 145
    Orange butter fougasse 68

'brouffade' from the River Rhône 84
'brouillade' with truffles 78

cabbage: potée d'amour 36
    large and small stuffed cabbages
        23
cakes: Auntie Lilette's strawberry
        cake 107-8
    caramel and apple cake 52
    chocolate cake 52
    fruit cake 48-50
    honey spice cake 53
    my cousin Jeanne's saint-honoré
        40-2
    my mother's almond log 75
    my strawberry cake 107
    Nanie's cake 148
    orange cake 53
    pear cake 28
    sultana cake 50-1
calissons 69
candied peel, orange and lemon 31
'capon', stuffed 133
cardoon tian 62-5
'Carthagène' 121
celeriac purée 87
celery with anchovies 61
chantilly puffs 196
cheese: Brousse cheese from Rove
        165
    cheese ravioli 101
    goats' cheese in olive oil 40
    'lou cachat' 119
cherry clafoutis 149
chicken: Mimosa Pastaga's sunshine
        chicken 195
    poached chicken 72
chickpeas, 'baïano' of 74
chicory compote 86
chocolate: chocolate cake 52
    hot chocolate 48
clams, spaghetti with 162
cod: salt cod, Grandet style 158
    salt cod with leeks 66-7

creamed salt cod tian 67
    'le grand aïoli' 184-5
    my mother's salt cod gratin 173
    salt cod bouillabaisse 131-2
coffee: my mother's almond log 75
courgettes: courgette gratin 176
    fritters 168-9
custard: snow cream 133-6
cuttlefish: fisherman's 'rouille' 114-16

daube from Avignon 80-1
dried fruit compote, Véronique L.'s
    90

eggs: 'brouillade' with truffles 78
    egg soup 78
    stuffed eggs 79
    see also omelettes

fennel: and tomatoes 158
    my godmother Lilou's compote 85
figs: fig gratin 181
    fig jam 165
fish: bouillabaisse 128-32
flowers, sugar 42
fougasse, Orange butter 68
fritters: acacia blossom 108
    courgette and courgette blossom
        168-9
    Madame Pavan's 'oreillettes' 89
fruit cake 48-50

gingerbread cream, Véronique L.'s
    90
grapes in eau-de-vie 70

honey spice cake 53

jam: fig 165
    green tomato 33
    rose-hip 55
    watermelon 121

kid, roast with anchovies 102

lamb: daube from Avignon 80-1
    leg with garlic cream sauce 102
    trotters and tripe bundles 178-9
lentils, New Year's Day 72-4
'lou cachat' 119

marmalade, bitter orange 55-6
meat: meat ravioli 101
    pot-au-feu 37
'meissounenco à la sucarello' 113-14
milk gratin 195
morels with pork sausages 104
mussels, ravioli with 101

navettes 162-3
nougat, black 68-9

octopus: spaghetti 'au monstre' 161
olives: broken olives 112
    olive bread 145
    pricked olives 112-13
    tapenade 125-6
omelettes: artichoke 100
    irreplaceable tomato 140
    omelette gâteau 188-92
    wild asparagus 95-6
Oraison gratin 27
Orange butter fougasse 68
oranges: Bernard's tabbouleh 192-3
    bitter orange marmalade 55-6
    candied orange and lemon peel 31
    Edith's orange and caramel salad 88
    orange cake 53
    orange wine 168
'oreillettes', Madame Pavan's 89

pasta: lumache pasta salad 146
pear cake 28
peppers, grilled aubergines and 119
persimmons with rum 30
pork: Catherine's roast with sage 38-9
    Oraison gratin 27
    pot-au-feu 37
potatoes: baked potatoes 26
    celeriac purée 87
    chips, Vinsobres style 154

the Countess' potatoes 106
fisherman's 'rouille' 114-16
mashed potatoes with leeks 86
Oraison gratin 27
a picturesque salad 117
potato and spinach tian 80
potatoes with bacon 26
poutargue, 125
pumpkin: pumpkin and bread soup 20
    pumpkin and rice tian 22
    pumpkin and spinach tian 21-2
    stuffed pumpkin 21

quince paste, Auntie Lilette's 27-8

rabbit: garlic rabbit 24
    rabbit sausage with olives 144
    rabbit terrine 141-4
    with mustard sauce 24
radish greens or nettle soup 173
ratatouille 187-8
ravioli: fried ravioli 127
    homemade ravioli 100-1
rice: Annie Laurent's rice pudding 120
    Rosette's rice pudding 87
rose-hip jam 55
rouille 129
'rouille', fisherman's 114-16

saint-honoré 40-2
salads: fisherman's 'rouille' 114-16
    green salad 96
    Joséphine salad 193
    lumache pasta salad 146
    a picturesque salad 117
    purple artichokes 100
    small salads 39
sauces: almond and anchovy 127
    almond and garlic 126
    l'anchoïade 141
    sauce rouge 38
    sauce verte 38
sausages, morels with pork 104
sea bream, the baron's 157
sea urchin 'rouille' 129
sea urchins 153

shortbread 136
snails: 'meissounenco à la sucarello' 113-14
snow cream 133-6
soups: 'l'aïgo boulido' 61
    Auntie Lilette's soupe au pistou 172
    egg soup 78
    pumpkin and bread soup 20
    radish greens or nettle soup 173
spaghetti: Auntie Anne's 162
    spaghetti 'au monstre' 161
    spaghetti with clams 162
spinach: spinach and pine nut tart 62
    spinach and sardine tian 79
strawberry cakes 107-8
sugar flowers 42
sultana cake 50-1

tapenade 125-6
tarts: simple apple tart 51
    spinach and pine nut tart 62
tellines à l'aïoli 116
thirteen desserts 70
toffee, my grandmother's Russian 31-3
tomatoes: green tomato jam 33
    irreplaceable tomato omelette 140
    tomato coulis 159
    tomato preserve 159
    tomatoes à la provençale 179
truffles: 'brouillade' with 78
    Lauris asparagus with 95
    truffle stew 65-6

vanilla crescents 56
vegetables: little green pies 185-6
    'les petits farcis' 176-7
    stew of spring vegetables 103

walnut wine, Olga's 168
watermelon jam 121
wine: 'Carthagène' 121
    Olga's walnut wine 168
    orange wine 168

ACKNOWLEDGEMENTS

~

It was while we were having dinner at home, in the kitchen with the *cigales* (cicadas), that Jean-Pierre and Christine Deméry convinced me to write this book, and today I am delighted to thank them for this excellent idea. My grandmother, my mother, my aunt Elisabeth, Mamie Rosette and Madame Cheynet, my cousin Jeanne and my godmother, Louise, have taught me everything I know. And I love them. But it is from my father, a hunter, a trout fisherman, a connoisseur of wine and good food, a man who could tell you stories about memorable meals that would make you drool, that I have inherited this passion for food, this pleasure in eating well, without which this book would probably never have been written.

My friends, Edith Mézard, Elisabeth Bourgeois, Martine Albertin, Lydie Laurent and Françoise Quinta, Monique and Jean-Claude Duveau, Annie Laurent, Véronique Lopez, Bruno Vaïarelli, Jo Guesde, Bernard Paul, Gérard Drouillet, 'Queen Jeanne', Eliane Jouve, Thierry Guien and Anne Sportiello, Hélène Feraud and Simone Rossi, Jérôme Couturier and Françoise de la Brosse, Thérèse Pavan, Françoise and Lionel Guin, have all frequently entertained me at their table before and during the preparation of this book. They have been its inspiration and its pleasure. I thank them for it.

My friends Ted and Lillian Williams, Jacques Grange, Géraud and Stéphanette de Sabran, Henri and Annie Laurent, Jean-Baptiste and Nicole Juge, Jean and Hélène Féraud, Michel and Edith Mézard, Bruno Carles, Gérard Drouillet and Denis Savon have been generous enough to lend me the enchanting places where we took the photographs for this book.

It is hard, probably impossible, to imagine the cataclysm that strikes a house when a team of photographers and stylists arrive. The furniture is piled up in the corridors, some windows are darkened with cloth while others are enhanced with silver reflectors. The floor is suddenly covered with crumpled bits of paper. Often, while you are shooting a lunch scene in the sun, nature gets in the way, clouds darken the sky so you have to bring out all the spotlights and their cables get merrily entangled. In the middle of all this mayhem, within the frame determined by Bernard Touillon's shrewd eye, the picture is being slowly organized, a picture which does not appear very clear to the untrained eye.

I thank them all for their patience and their trust, and I hope Bernard's beautiful photos will have totally reassured them by now.

How could I forget to thank Ariane and Gérard Blanc for letting me use their lovely yellow china for so long, as well as Bernard Paul and Bruno Carles of *l'Espace Béchard*, and Maria Giancatarina and Jean-Claude Clément of *Quai de la Gare* in l'Isle-sur-la-Sorgue, who kindly lent me part of their collections, and of course, my dear Edith Mézard who, often at the very last minute, embroidered, sewed or ironed the table-cloths for this book.

My thanks also to Philippe Baique, the wine waiter at the *Mas de Tourteron* in Gordes, who advised me so expertly and cleverly about the choice of wines.

I certainly would not want to forget Francette Drin, who has been so helpful with her kind and thoughtful advice. Thanks to her, this book has gained its clarity.

Finally, this work has taken shape thanks to the experience and the talent of Ghislaine Bavoillot, Marc Walter and Florence Picard.